Sage

Accounting

2000

David Weale

**Bernard Babani (Publishing) Ltd
The Grampians
Shepherds Bush Road
London W6 7NF
England**

Please Note

Although every care has been taken with the production of this book to ensure that any instructions or any of the other contents operate in a correct and safe manner, the Author and the Publishers do not accept any responsibility for any failure, damage or loss caused by following the said contents. The Author and Publisher do not take any responsibility for errors or omissions.

The Author and Publisher make no warranty or representation, either express or implied, with respect to the contents of this book, its quality, merchantability or fitness for a particular purpose.

The Author and Publisher will not be liable to the purchaser or to any other person or legal entity with respect to any liability, loss or damage (whether direct, indirect, special, incidental or consequential) caused or alleged to be caused directly or indirectly by this book.

The book is sold as is, without any warranty of any kind, either expressed or implied, respecting the contents, including but not limited to implied warranties regarding the book's quality, performance, correctness or fitness for any particular purpose.

No part of this book may be reproduced or copied by any means whatever without written permission of the publisher.

© 1999 BERNARD BABANI (publishing) LTD

First Published - November 1999

British Library Cataloguing in Publication Data

A catalogue record for this book is available from the British Library

ISBN 0 85934 482 7

Cover Design by Gregor Arthur

Cover Illustration by Adam Willis

Printed and bound in Great Britain by Bath Press

Contents

Trademarks

Microsoft® and Windows® are registered trademarks of Microsoft® Corporation.

All other trademarks are the registered and legally protected trademarks of the companies who make the products. There is no intent to use the trademarks generally and readers should investigate ownership of a trademark before using it for any purpose.

About the author

David Weale is a Fellow of the Institute of Chartered Accountants and has worked in both private and public practice. At present, he is a lecturer in business computing.

Introduction

This book is intended to explain how to make use of Sage Instant Accounting and to help the user to understand the program.

It could be used by anyone having bought the program who wants a simple explanatory text or by someone thinking of buying the program who wants to see how it works.

Sage Instant Accounting is designed to be a simple to use and very effective financial tool for your business.

It contains many of the features found in the more sophisticated Sage Line 50 programs (although some of the features within Instant Accounting offer fewer options). The data you enter will be usable if you upgrade to Line 50 at any time and you will find that Line 50 is similar to Instant Accounting in use.

For the purposes of this book it is assumed that the reader is familiar with the WINDOWS environment. If you are not, then you need to consult the WINDOWS manual or a book on the subject or attend a course.

I hope you enjoy it.

David Weale November 1999

Accounting Terminology

If you are new to the idea of accounts or unclear about some of the specialised terms used then this section will help.

I have explained the terms used in accounting so that you can see how Sage Instant Accounting fits into the accounting framework.

To begin we will look at the accounts produced by the program, this is followed by an explanation of the ledgers, double-entry bookkeeping, VAT accounting and other useful techniques used within the program.

The Accounts

Profit & Loss Account

This shows how successful your business is over a specified time (for example a year).

From the **Sales** are deducted the **Purchases,** the result is called the **Gross Profit**.

Then all the **overheads** you have incurred during the period are listed, totalled and deducted from the **Gross Profit**. The resulting figure is called the **Net Profit**.

This can be produced as often as you wish, for example monthly or yearly. The profit (or loss) shows how well the business has traded.

Date: 24/08/1999	**HiFi Supplies (Weymouth)**		Page: 1
Time: 11:25:27	**Profit & Loss**		

From: Month 1, January 1999
To: Month 2, February 1999

Chart of Accounts: Default Chart of Accounts

	Period		Year to Date	
Sales				
Product Sales	885.00		885.00	
		885.00		885.00
Purchases				
Purchases	2,917.00		2,917.00	
		2,917.00		2,917.00
Direct Expenses				
		0.00		0.00
Gross Profit/(Loss):		(2,032.00)		(2,032.00)
Overheads				
		0.00		0.00
Net Profit/(Loss):		(2,032.00)		(2,032.00)

Balance Sheet

Unlike the Profit & Loss Account that covers a period of time, the Balance Sheet shows the assets, liabilities and capital of your business at a specific date.

The **Year To** figures are the cumulative figures for the year to date.

```
Date:    24/08/1999           HiFi Supplies (Weymouth)              Page:   1
Time:    11:27:00                  Balance Sheet

From:    Month 1, January 1999
To:      Month 2, February 1999

Chart of Account:                Default Chart of Accounts

                                    Period                    Year to Date
Fixed Assets
                                              0.00                        0.00
Current Assets
Debtors                            493.50                     493.50
VAT Liability                      355.60                     355.60
                                            849.10                      849.10
Current Liabilities
Creditors : Short Term           1,594.48                   1,594.48
Bank Account                     1,286.62                   1,286.62
                                          2,881.10                    2,881.10
      Current Assets less Current Liabilities:   (2,032.00)             (2,032.00)
        Total Assets less Current Liabilities:   (2,032.00)             (2,032.00)
Long Term Liabilities
                                              0.00                        0.00
        Total Assets less Total Liabilities:     (2,032.00)             (2,032.00)
Capital & Reserves
P&L Account                       (2,032.00)                 (2,032.00)
                                          (2,032.00)                   (2,032.00)
```

Assets are the items your business owns and **Liabilities** are the items or amount your business owes to others.

Assets are divided into two types, Fixed and Current.

5

Fixed Assets

Normally these are assets that will be retained for some time; examples are buildings (property), office equipment.

Current Assets

Assets that are temporary in nature, for example bank accounts, cash, debtors (customers who owe you money).

Liabilities

Amounts due to others.

Net Assets

This represents the difference between total assets and total liabilities.

Financed By

This represents the money invested by you in the business **plus** the accumulated profits (reserves) and the profit or loss for the period.

By definition a Balance Sheet **must** balance, for example the **Net Assets** must be equal to the total of the **Financed By** section. Luckily with computerised accounts it is difficult not to balance.

The Ledgers

The day-to-day transactions of a business are recorded in ledgers. There are three main ledgers, Sales, Purchases and Nominal.

Sales Ledger

Sage calls this **Customers** which is a more sensible description.

This ledger records all the transactions with your individual customers. A separate account within the ledger is opened for each customer and all transactions for that customer are recorded in that account, for example invoices sent to the customer, credit notes and payments from the customer.

The balance on the customer's account represents the amount the customer owes to you.

The total of all the balances in all the customer accounts represents the total debtors' figure and is shown as the **Debtors Control Account** in the **Nominal** ledger.

Purchase Ledger

Again **Sage** has renamed this as **Suppliers** and it is used to record your transactions with each of your suppliers.

It operates in a very similar way to the **Sales** ledger and the total of all the balances on all the individual supplier accounts is the **Creditors Control Account**. This represents the total amount you owe to your suppliers at any time.

Nominal Ledger

This summarises all the financial data from the **Sales** and **Purchase** ledgers and from other financial records such as the cashbook and bank.

The **Trial Balance** is made up from the balances of the individual nominal ledger accounts and is used to produce the Profit & Loss Account and the Balance Sheet.

Double-Entry Accounting

All accounting systems whether manual or computerised use the **double-entry system** to record transactions. This means that all data is recorded twice, once as a debit and once as a credit entry (in different accounts).

With computerised systems the mechanics of the double-entry system are carried out automatically and the system is therefore self balancing. When you look at some of the statements and reports generated by SAGE you will see two columns, the left headed **DB** or **Debit** and the right **CR** or **Credit**.

VAT

All businesses with a certain turnover have to register with the Customs & Excise for VAT. When you register you are allocated a VAT Registration number that you must quote on all your documentation.

If registered you must charge VAT on all goods or services (that are chargeable to VAT - not all are) and you can set against this all VAT you pay on goods or services supplied to you.

The difference between the Input and Output VAT has to be paid to the C&E (or possibly reclaimed).

Budgets

Once you have entered the data into the program then as well as producing the accounts you can produce information that may help you manage your business more effectively.

A method of keeping control of your finances is to use budgets. You set budgets for any or all of your different types of income and expenditure. These budgets can be set using the previous year's figures or estimates that you have made. As the year progresses you can look at reports showing the budgeted and the actual figures with the difference or variance between budget and actual also shown.

The advantage of this is being able quickly to see where you have large differences between budget and actual and then being able to do something about it before it is too late.

Bank Reconciliations

You can reconcile the figures in your computerised accounts against the actual bank statements to ensure that the bank statement is correct. You can add any necessary items to the computerised system, for example bank charges.

Credit Control

Another feature that enables you to manage your business better is credit control. This allows you to set credit limits and to monitor your customer accounts so that you may not get in the situation where a customer owes you too much money for too long a period.

Operating Conventions

Standard Windows buttons

Microsoft Windows 95/98 lets you alter the size of the active window; there are four buttons, which appear on every window.

Clicking on this button closes down the program (you will be asked if you want to save any changes that you have made to the file).

This reduces the size of the window to its previous size. This button is an alternative to the next one.

This button enlarges the active (current) window to fill the screen.

This button minimises the window, if you do this you will see the program name appearing along the Windows 95/98 **Start bar** at the bottom of the screen. You can click on the program name to activate it.

The Initial Screen

When you load Sage Instant Accounting 2000, you will see the main screen.

This contains the module buttons and the pull-down menus.

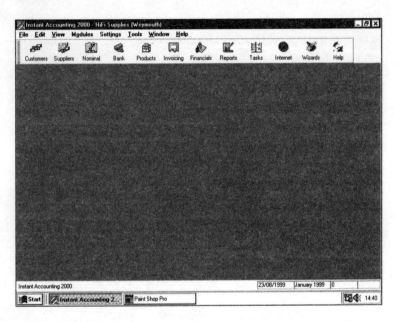

Some screens have an arrow button on the right; clicking this enables you to see the other available buttons on the toolbar.

Using the scroll bars

Some of the dialog boxes have vertical scroll bars, these have an arrow at the top and bottom and you click on the arrows to move up or down the list shown within the dialog box.

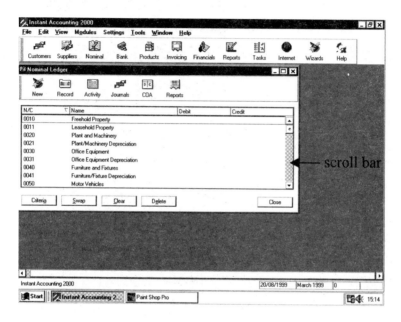

Horizontal scroll bars also appear along the bottom of some windows and dialog boxes.

Selecting records

You may want to look at or alter the details of certain of your customers or suppliers. Many of the dialog boxes display a list of items, for example customer names or nominal codes.

You can select any of these by clicking the mouse pointer on them.

To select more than one simply click again and you will see that both are highlighted (and so on if you want to select more).

To alter the selection you can deselect by clicking the mouse on the item again.

To sort the data double-click the mouse pointer on the heading of the column you want sorted (hold the **Shift** key down at the same time for a reverse order sort). The sorted data will revert to its original state when you close down the window.

Moving around the dialog boxes

When you enter data or other details within any of the screens you can use the following techniques.

❖ Within each dialog box you use either click the mouse or you can **Tab** between each field.

❖ To move up (or backwards) within the dialog box hold down the **Shift** key and then press the **Tab** key.

Function Keys

Sage makes use of the function keys on your keyboard; here is a table of them.

F1	Brings up the HELP screens
F2	Displays the calculator
F4	Displays a list of alternate choices e.g. A/C codes
F6	Repeats the data from the previous row
F11	Loads the WINDOWS Control Panel
F12	Loads the Report Designer

Some words of warning

Always back up your data files on a regular basis.

This book is not a substitute for reading the manual, it cannot contain the detailed explanations that are contained in the manual and indeed is not intended to. Read the manual if you are at all confused or unsure about any activity.

Always practise before entering real data to allow you to try out techniques to see the effect they have.

Do **not** enter data unless you are clear about what will happen to your accounts as a result of entering that data.

Run parallel systems (manual and computer) until you are very confident that the computer system is functioning satisfactorily.

Start with a small section of your accounts on the computer to gain confidence and experience, for example the sales ledger.

Use your accountant's knowledge and skill to help you.

Consider subscribing to the **Sage** help line. This is very useful, you can phone for any help you need and will get information about upgrades.

The Welcome Screen

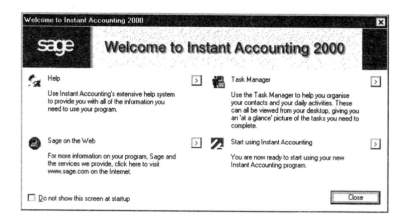

The original screen, you can avoid this appearing again by ticking the **Do not show this screen at startup** box.

The options available here are explained later where necessary.

The Pull Down Menus

This section explains the variety of commands available within the pull down menus.

Clicking on any of the menus titles displays a (pull down) menu. From the list you select the command you want.

Within each pull down menu you select the command you want by clicking on it with the mouse or by moving the cursor onto it by using the cursor control keys and then pressing the **Return** key.

File Menu

Open Demo **D**ata
Backup...
Restore...
Maintenance...
Send Mail...
Run Easy Startup **W**izard
E**x**it

From this you have the following choices.

Open Demo Data

This opens data created for you by Sage so that you can practise and see how the various screens and reports appear.

Backup and Restore

These are **very** different and if you confuse them, you could end up in a terrible mess.

It is **essential** that you back up your data files; if anything happened to these your business could rapidly become a disaster area. The most effective security is to regularly back up your data files.

This could work based on keeping **at least** three generations of backups.

Each set of backup files should be kept in a separate location (at least one being kept away from the office).

Always **label** the backup discs clearly

The generations may work like this:

❖   A backup is made using a new set of discs

❖   Next day another backup is made

❖   The following day a third backup is made

❖   The fourth day the first backup is re-used

❖   The fifth day the second backup is re-used.

A weekly backup can also made on the same principles as above

So whether you choose to back up daily or weekly (or in between) you are keeping three sets of backups on the go.

Another possibility is to keep a daily backup for a week (five sets) and a weekly backup for the last four weeks and a monthly backup for the last six months (or whatever permutations you choose).

The **Restore** option lets you replace corrupted files (or to replace horrible mistakes) with the last version of your files that you backed up.

There is a considerable difference between **Backup** and **Restore**; if you confuse them then you could end up with no data files at all.

If you want to know more about folders and their structure any good book on Windows will help.

Backup

This copies the data from your hard disc onto a floppy disc or zip drive.

It is **vital** to back up your data files regularly and you will be prompted to do so when exiting the program.

You can back up at any time by pulling down the **File** menu and selecting **Backup**.

Whichever method you use, the first screen you see is shown below.

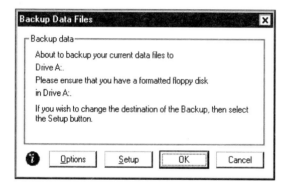

Click the **Setup** button and then choose the **A:** drive (or whatever drive/folder you wish to back up to).

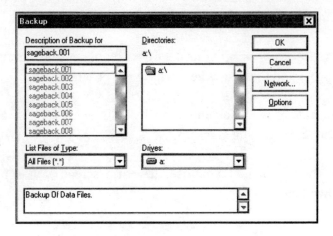

Finally click on **OK**.

The files are saved as **sageback.001**.

However they is nothing to prevent you saving your backup files as **sageback.002**, **sageback.003**, etc., so that you have several different versions of the backup each saved at different stages of entering the data.

I suggest backing up to a floppy disc, zip drive, or tape streamer, etc.

It is important **not** to back up to the same hard disc your data is currently held on (usually the **C:** drive).

26

The whole point of backing up is to have viable data files to restore from if the original files are corrupted or lost, e.g. if the hard disc becomes unreadable (in which case the backups are likely to be irretrievable if saved to that same hard disc).

The Options button

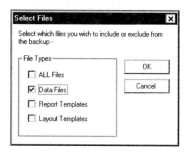

The default is only to back up the data files; if you want to back up any of the other file types then you need to click (tick) the relevant boxes.

Restore

This is the opposite of backing up, when you restore from the floppy disc, you are copying the (backed up) data from the floppy disc to the hard drive, writing over (replacing) the original data files.

The first screen looks like this.

Please read the warning carefully!

If you want to restore from a backup file other than **sageback.001**, then you need to click on the **Setup** button in order to select a different file.

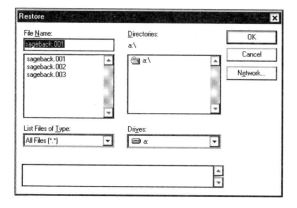

Select the file you want to restore and click **OK**.

Maintenance

Correcting Mistakes

One of the most common problems is knowing how to correct mistakes or errors. We all make mistakes now and again.

What follows is a guide to the correction of errors.

The majority of mistakes can be corrected using the **File** (pull down menu) and selecting **Maintenance**. As you can see from the illustration, there are four alternatives.

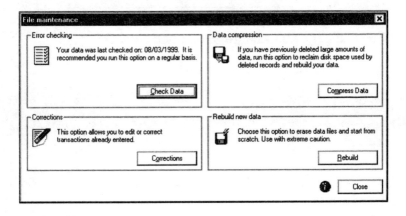

There are some errors or mistakes which require a journal entry to correct, or are mistakes to do with the stock (**Products**), which have to be adjusted within the **Products** module.

Error checking

This checks the data you have entered for inconsistencies or corruption.

Once you have run this you will see a report detailing any problems encountered.

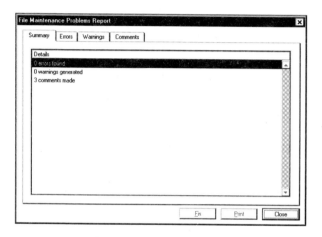

You can use the **Fix** button (if available for the particular problem) to remedy the situation.

The kind of errors that occur include values outside the limits set by the program, transactions that do not match properly, missing or corrupt files or invalid nominal codes.

Warnings

More serious than comments, these should be investigated and dealt with.

Errors

The most serious type of problem, these require fixing.

Comments

These are the least serious, usually the result of an inconsistency in the data.

Corrections

If you have entered data incorrectly, it is often possible to correct the individual item by using this button.

You will see a list of all the transactions and you highlight the one you want to correct and then **Edit** it.

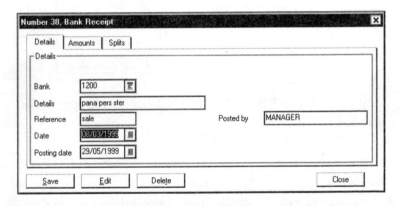

Unfortunately, not all errors can be corrected in this way.

Deleted items are shown in red in the audit trail.

Data compression

This clears space on your disc previously occupied by data you have deleted.

Rebuild new data

Be very careful with this, you will clear your data (so you can begin again).

Ideal when practising but not necessarily a good idea otherwise.

Send Mail

This loads up your email editor.

Run Easy Startup Wizard

This runs the startup wizard.

Exit

When you want to exit from **Sage**, you will be prompted to back up the data if you have made any changes.

Edit Menu

Cut	
Copy	
Paste	
Insert Row	(F7)
Delete Row	(F8)
Duplicate Cell	(F6)

The standard commands, however note the bottom three, which let you use the function keys within **Sage**, as a quicker alternative.

View Menu

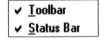

You can choose to display the toolbar and status bars (the default) or remove them by removing the ticks.

Modules Menu

```
Customers...
Suppliers...
Nominal Ledger...
Bank...
Products...
Invoicing...
Financials...
Sage Report Writer...
Task Manager...
Internet Browser
Wizards               ▶
```

This menu is an alternative to the use of the toolbar buttons to select the modules.

Settings Menu

```
Company Preferences...
Customer Defaults...
Supplier Defaults...
Product Defaults...
Invoice Defaults...

Financial Year...
Change Program Date...

Tax Codes...
Currency...
Departments...
Product Categories...
Control Accounts...
Finance Rates...

Change Password...
```

These are the original settings that come with **Sage**. You can alter them if you so wish and then your new settings become the defaults. Most of the original settings can be altered or set when you use the **Easy Startup Wizard**.

Company Preferences

These are set when you install the program or create a new company. As you can see from the illustration, the screen shows the name, address, etc., any of which you can alter.

Customer Defaults

Selecting this allows you to alter the default settings for customers.

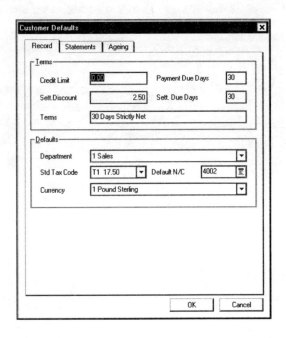

It is sensible to set up the defaults for the most used data and then you only have to alter some of the individual accounts.

You can alter any of these and they will appear automatically on every customer account you set up, you can also change them on an individual basis as necessary by altering the settings within the individual account in the appropriate ledger.

Supplier Defaults

The same comments apply to this and the **Product** and **Invoice Defaults** as to the Customer Defaults above. The latter screens are shown for reference.

Product Defaults

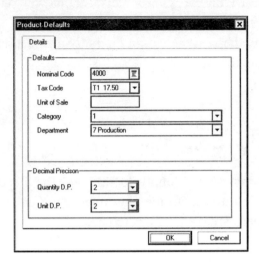

Invoice Defaults

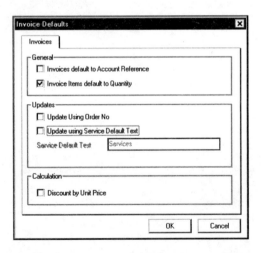

Financial Year

To check this, pull down the **Settings** menu and select **Financial Year**, you should see the dialog box shown below; alter the date to that shown (if necessary).

You can alter the start of the financial year, but only if you have not entered any financial data.

Change Program Date

This is the system date; you can change it if necessary, but remember to change it back afterwards.

Tax Codes

This displays a dialog box that allows you to alter the codes and the VAT rate applicable to them.

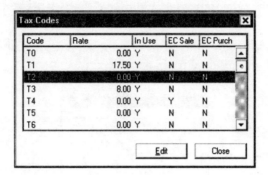

To change any of the codes highlight them and then click on the **Edit** button.

You can enter the details and then click on OK to save it. You should then see the relevant figures and selections change within the VAT Code Setup box.

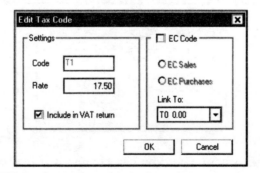

On installation, Instant Accounting automatically sets up the following VAT Rates for you

T0	zero rated
T1	standard rate
T2	exempt
T4	standard rate sales to EC customers
T7	zero rate purchases from EC
T8	standard rate purchases from EC
T9	non vat transactions

Currency

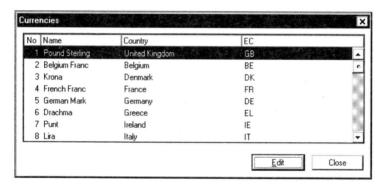

You can alter any of these by using the **Edit** button.

Departments

Here you can set up the departmental structure you want.

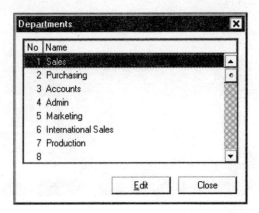

To create departments simply click on the number and then on the **Edit** button. Enter the name you want to call the department and then on the OK button and you will see it included in the list.

Product Categories

This works in a very similar way to **Departments.**

Control Accounts

You can alter the code for any of the displayed control accounts, however I would think very seriously before doing so.

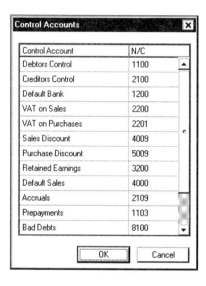

You cannot alter the code for most control accounts once any data has been entered.

Finance Rates

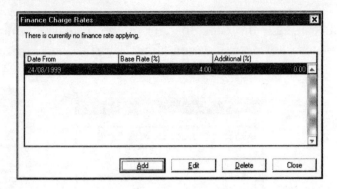

You can set the **Finance Rate**, for example if you want to charge customers for late payment of invoices (see **Charges** in the **Customers** module).

Change Password

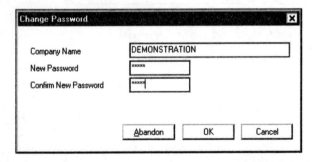

If you do set a password, you must remember it!

Tools menu

Global Changes...
Convert Data...
Upgrade Program
Period End ▸
Options...

Global Changes

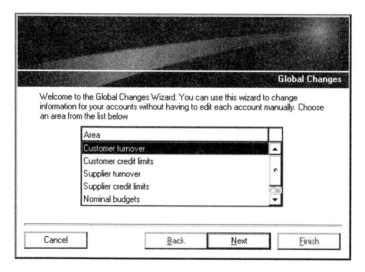

Global Changes

Welcome to the Global Changes Wizard. You can use this wizard to change
information for your accounts without having to edit each account manually. Choose
an area from the list below

Area
Customer turnover
Customer credit limits
Supplier turnover
Supplier credit limits
Nominal budgets

Cancel   Back   Next   Finish

You can make global changes to the various settings from
this option.

Convert Data

This enables you to convert data from a previous version of the program.

Upgrade program

This connects you to the Sage web site so that you can upgrade your version.

Period End

This has three options.

```
Clear Audit Trail...
Month End...
Year End...
```

Clear Audit Trail

You can clear the Audit trail of certain completed transactions, i.e. reconciled and fully paid transactions.

Month End

This sets the **Month to date turnover** figures to zero in the supplier and customer records.

Year End

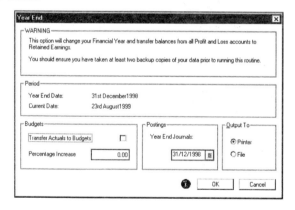

You can set budgets using the actual figures or a percentage increase.

Transfer Actuals to Budgets
This allows you to set the actual figures spent this year as
the budget for next, optionally setting a percentage increase
for next year's budgets (**Percentage Increase**).

Options

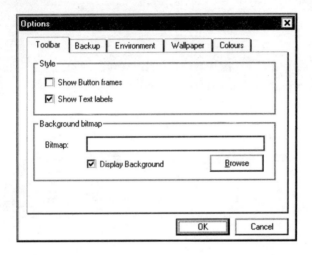

You can use this to set various system settings within **Sage**.

Window menu

These are standard WINDOWS commands that arrange the (open) windows on the screen.

```
Tile
Cascade
Arrange Icons
Minimise All
Close All
```

The one that I find most useful is **Close All**, which closes all the open windows.

Help menu

<u>H</u>elp Contents
<u>L</u>ibrary Contents
<u>S</u>hortcut Keys
<u>A</u>bout Instant Accounting 2000...

These are organised in a similar way to other Windows
programs with hypertext links.

The help screens are accessed by either pulling
down the **Help** menu or by clicking the **Help**
button at the end of the main toolbar.

You can also use the **F12** function key.

How to find help

Initially you choose either the **Help Contents** or **Library
Contents** from the choices.

Help

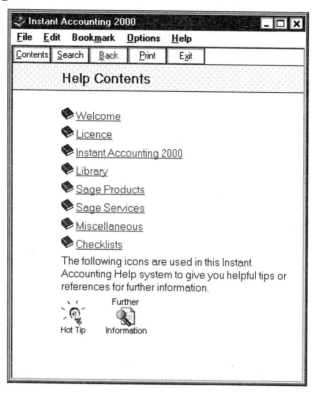

Library

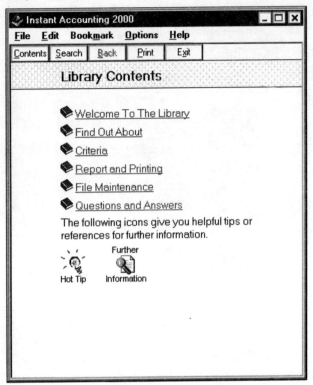

If you click on any of the topics listed (on either of the two previous screens) you will obtain a further list of topics (which are also clickable to either get another list of topics or to display the relevant help screen).

An example of the topics lists is shown below.

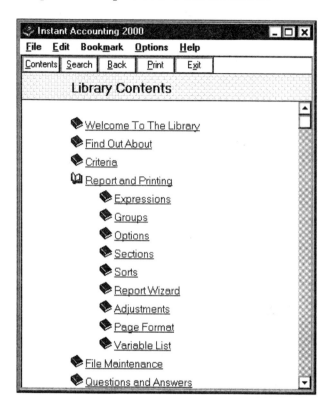

One of the actual help screens is illustrated on the next page, many help screens contain hyperlinks which you can click to go to another topic or which explain a word or phrase.

Links are normally shown in green and underlined.

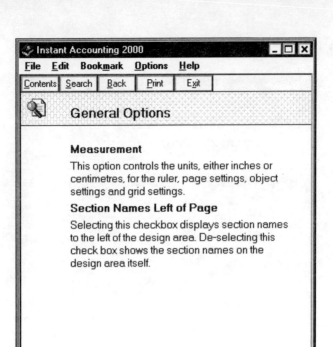

Measurement

This option controls the units, either inches or centimetres, for the ruler, page settings, object settings and grid settings.

Section Names Left of Page

Selecting this checkbox displays section names to the left of the design area. De-selecting this check box shows the section names on the design area itself.

Using the Search button

Along the top of the **Help** or **Library Contents** are a series
of buttons, one of which is the **Search** button.

You can search for keywords (as opposed to working
through the lists within the **Help** or **Library Contents**
screens). If you click on the **Search** button, you will
display the following dialog box.

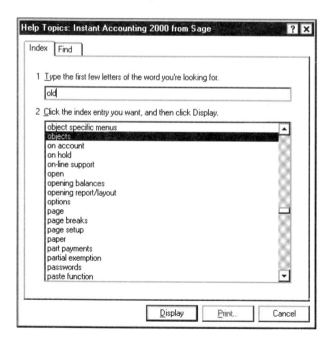

You enter the keyword(s) and the program will find the topic closest to the word(s) you entered. Then click the **Display** button and you will see the help on that topic.

Personally I find the **Index** search quick and easy, however for certain topics the **Find** search is more exhaustive and effective if slightly slower in execution.

Shortcut Keys

Remember these, as they will allow you to carry out these activities more quickly than using the toolbar buttons or menus.

The toolbar buttons

As you can see from the toolbar (illustrated above) the program contains various modules, which are explained below.

Customers

You enter customer details, record invoices and produce reports, keep track of how much you are owed and how long the money has been owed to you.

The **Customers** option is the Sage equivalent of the **Sales** ledger. The **Customers** toolbar is shown below.

We will look at each of these buttons briefly.

New

This begins the customers' section of the **Easy Startup Wizard**.

Record

This option lets you set up the details for each customer. You can enter specific details for the customer by clicking on the various tabs along the top of the dialog box, e.g. **Credit Control**.

These details take precedence over the global settings you may have entered when using the **Easy Startup Wizard** originally.

Some items are described below.

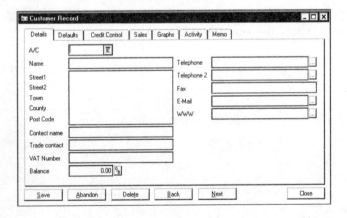

A/C

Each customer must be allocated an A/C code. This code will be used throughout the program.

Each code must be unique (in fact if you try to use an already existing code the screen will fill up with the details you have entered for that code).

Considerable thought should be given to the allocation of account codes, the more carefully and logically you do this, the more structured and workable your system will be.

It is always worthwhile arranging the structure so that you can easily add new customers when necessary.

Account codes can be made up of any combination of letters and numbers.

Nominal

The sales code for that customer, at present it is set for 4000 but can be altered to any sales code you may wish.

Graph

You can produce (and alter) graphs based upon the transactions for any customer.

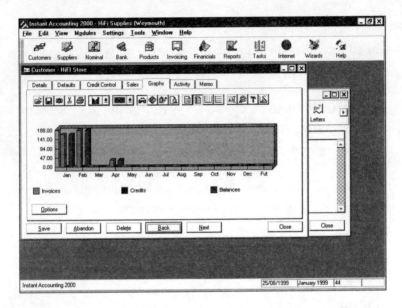

Activity

This displays the transactions that have taken place on that account.

Aged

The aged display will show the amount owing for each account aged over several different periods.

Invoice

A/C

This is the account code for the customer (click on the magnifying glass button to display all the existing codes). The name of the customer is then automatically entered.

Date

By default this is the system date but it can be altered as necessary, be careful to make sure this is correct as it will affect the reports and financial statements.

Amount

Enter the amount and the VAT will be calculated (remember to check the VAT rate is correct for that item). The total column will be calculated and also the cumulative total.

The Calculate Net button

Very useful, if you have entered the gross amount, you can click on this button and the VAT will be calculated on the amount and the program will **deduct** the VAT. This could be used if you are only given the amount inclusive of VAT

Adding items to the invoice

Simply TAB onto the next line of the form and continue as before. You are not limited to the number of items shown initially as you can carry on below.

Credit Note

This is the opposite of the Invoice option and the entries are made in the same way.

Charges

Before you can use this to charge your customers for outstanding amounts, you need to set the rates by pulling down the **Settings** menu and selecting **Finance Rates**.

You can then start the **Credit Charges Information** wizard by clicking the **Charges** button on the toolbar.

The wizard takes you through various choices about customers and transactions which you want to add charges to.

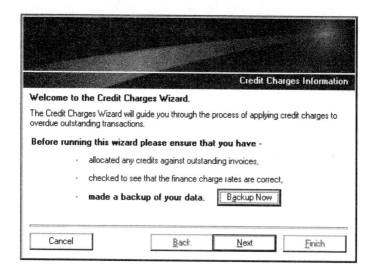

Welcome to the Credit Charges Wizard.

The Credit Charges Wizard will guide you through the process of applying credit charges to overdue outstanding transactions.

Before running this wizard please ensure that you have -

- allocated any credits against outstanding invoices,

- checked to see that the finance charge rates are correct,

- **made a backup of your data.** [Backup Now]

[Cancel]   [Back] [Next]   [Finish]

Labels

You can print labels to your customers by selecting this option. You can preview the labels; send them to a printer or to a file for future use.

Letters

You can generate a letter requesting payment of an overdue amount or you create your own letters.

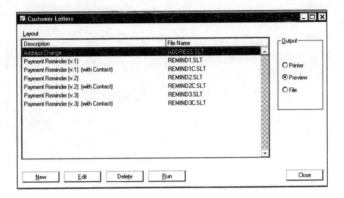

Creating your own letters

This is easy to do and involves using the **New** button within the Letters option.

You simply select the variables you want to include within your letter, add the text and save it. The new letter will be available whenever you need it.

Statement

This generates a statement for the selected customers.

Report

The initial screen lets you choose from several different reports.

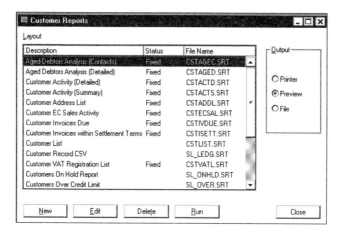

Edit

This option loads whatever report file you have highlighted from the list. You can then alter the file and save it in its new version. You cannot edit the fixed reports.

Run

This will merge the chosen report with the highlighted customers in the box displaying the customers. If no customers are highlighted then all will be included in the report.

Suppliers

Similar to Customers, you keep details of your suppliers and how much you owe to them, for how long.

This is the **Purchase** ledger in traditional accounting systems.

Nominal

This option keeps track of all transactions that are allocated to the different codes you are using.

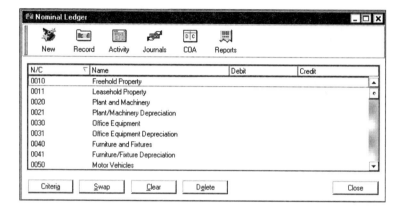

The display shows a list of the Nominal Accounts.

If you add codes, make sure they are within the correct range for the activity (for example Sales codes are in the 4000 - 4999 range).

Record

You can then add a new code or alter data about that account (for example the name you want to call the account) by selecting the **Record** button or the **New** button (if you prefer to use the wizard).

Activity

This shows the transactions that have taken place within the selected nominal code.

Journals

A journal is used to make adjustments to the data you have entered, for example to adjust for **Suspense** accounts. This is where knowledge of double entry techniques can be useful.

The data entry screen looks like this.

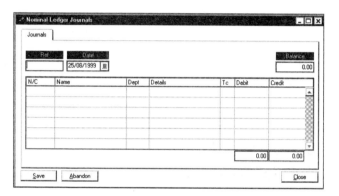

You cannot finish or save a journal unless the cumulative total for the debit column is the same as the cumulative total for the credit column, e.g. the balance is zero.

The **date** for the journal entry (as for all entries) is very important as **Sage** groups data according to the date of the transaction.

COA

This is a summary of the various groupings of the nominal codes. Click the **COA** button and then the **Edit** button.

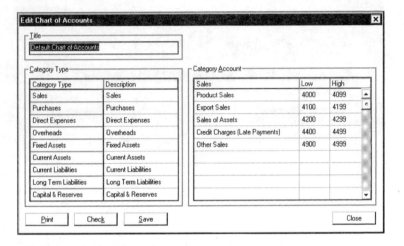

You can alter the descriptions and the low and high parameters for each range. You can add new codes to the list, however be very careful to make sure that they are within the correct category, e.g. all overheads are between code 7000 and 9999.

Reports

You can display, edit the existing reports or create your own.

Bank

You use this option to record all moneys paid or received by you. It can also be used for credit card transactions and for cash transactions.

This deals with the bank accounts of your business. The following screen will be displayed.

You can set up separate bank accounts for different credit card companies you deal with and set up a bank account for cash transactions and these can be reconciled.

Reconciling the bank

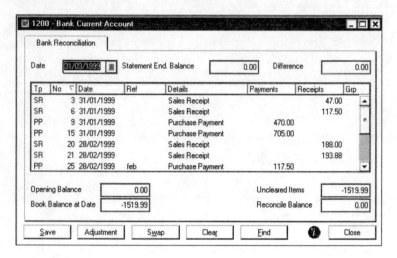

All transactions that have been entered into the computer will be shown for the chosen bank account (only one bank account can be shown at any one time).

The idea is that you reconcile or agree the transactions on your real bank account with those in your computer, by adding additional transactions to adjust for bank charges, interest and any other items that have not been entered into the computer.

How to reconcile

Click on the **Reconcile** button, this will display all the recorded transactions in the chosen bank account.

Set the date to the date of the Bank Statement.

In the **Statement End Balance** box enter the balance on the bank statement.

Check the opening balance is the same as that on the bank statement (as it should be if you reconciled correctly last month).

Go through your bank statement checking each item against the screen. Select (highlight) each identical item.

Any incorrect items should be altered and any items on the bank statement which do not appear on the screen, e.g. bank charges should be entered.

Make sure the balances on the screen now are equal to the bank balance on your statement and save the reconciliation.

The only items, which will show up next time, are those which appeared on the screen but not on the bank statement i.e. those that had been banked but had not been cleared.

Credit card receipts

Nowadays many businesses accept credit cards for sales and you can use one or more of the bank accounts to deal with these transactions.

Payment/Receipt

Used to record payments or income where there has not been an account created in the **Customer** or **Supplier** modules.

Customer/Supplier

Used to record bank or cash payments from customers or to suppliers who have accounts created for them in the **Customer** or **Supplier** modules.

Transfer

This enables you to transfer money from one bank account to another.

Recurring

This lets you deal with recurring entries; the data entry screen is shown below.

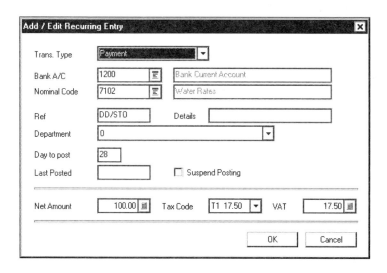

Statement

You can preview, print or send the bank statement to a file for future use.

Reports

This contains reports specific to this module.

Products

Here your stock details are recorded. You can see the items you hold in stock and their prices.

Details from this are used in the Invoicing option to print your invoices.

New/Record

You can add new stock items.

Reports

There is a limited range of existing reports.

Invoicing

To produce invoices for your customers you use this option, you can also automatically update the Sales (Customers) Ledger.

Product Service Credit SrvCredit Print Update Reports

Product/Service

Within this you can produce invoices for customers from your stock records or for services supplied.

The data entry screen looks like this.

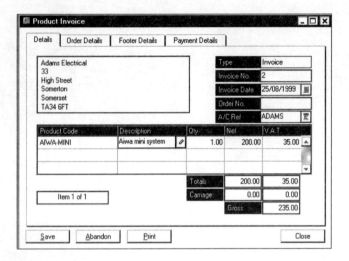

Credit Note/SrvCredit

If you have stock items returned to you and you want to issue a credit note to your customer then select this option.

You should make sure the codes are the same as the original.

Print

You can print invoices for selected customers.

Update

It is very important to use this button, as your ledgers will not be updated otherwise. This process generates a report that will tell you if the invoice has not been posted and why, it is best to print this report and read it.

Note that you can only update an invoice to the ledger once.

Financials

This is where you print or view your accounts, set budgets and calculate your VAT return or compare this year's figures with last year's. This information is vital for the successful management of your financial affairs.

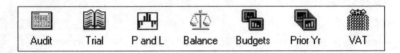

Audit   Trial   P and L   Balance   Budgets   Prior Yr   VAT

Audit

One of the most important reports you can produce is the audit trail; this is a list of the items that have been recorded (including any corrections you have made). It is used by auditors, etc., to ensure that your accounts are correct and not e.g. fraudulent.

You are given a choice of several versions.

An example of the brief audit trail is on the next page.

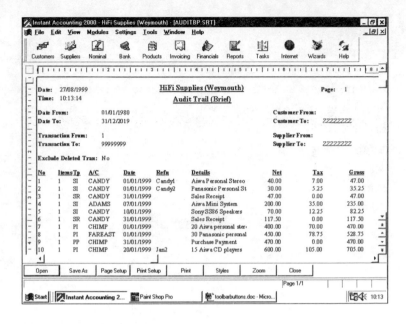

The audit trail transaction types are shown below.

SI	Sales invoice
SC	Sales credit
SA	Sales on account
SD	Sales discount
SR	Sales receipt
PI	Purchase invoice
PC	Purchase credit
PA	Purchase on account
PD	Purchase discount
PP	Purchase payment
BP	Bank payment
BR	Bank receipt
CR	Cash receipt
CP	Cash payment
JD	Journal debit
JC	Journal credit

Trial (Balance)

This lists the balances on the different nominal ledger accounts containing data from transactions.

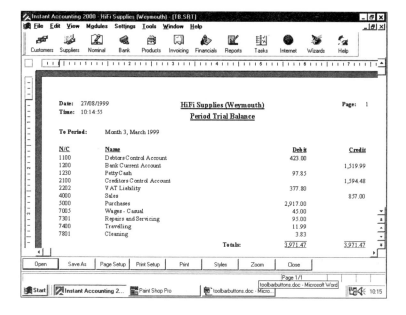

P & L / Balance (Sheet)

The display shows the selected month and the cumulative
figures for the year to date.

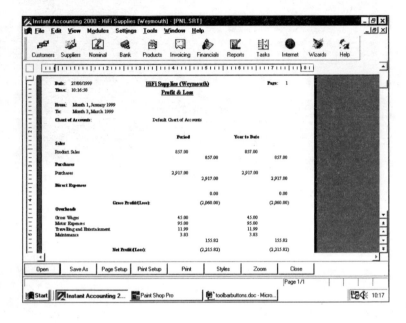

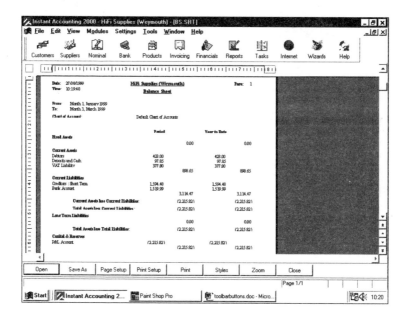

Budgets/Prior Yr

This produces a monthly report of the budget, the actual figures and the variance (difference between the actual and budgeted figures) for both the selected month and the year to date.

Before you can get any meaningful information from this report, you will need to have set up the original budgets, to do so you enter the budget figures in each nominal account record (**Nominal**, **Record**).

VAT Return

Your VAT return will be calculated automatically for you if you use this option. The choices are:

Calculate

You will need to click on the **Calculate** button to make the program look through the transactions for the period and produce a VAT return for you.

Reconcile

This sets a flag (or marker) to the items included within the current VAT return. This means that they will not be included again unless you want them to be by clicking on the **Include Reconciled Transactions** button.

You can look at the detailed breakdown of each figure by clicking in the appropriate box and a screen showing the breakdown will be displayed.

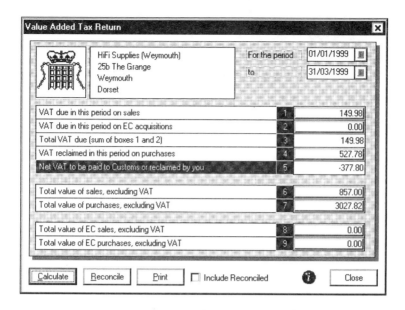

It is suggested that you **zero** the tax control accounts at the end of each month (or every three months). This will mean that you are only dealing with one month's figures at a time and will, therefore, find the task of reconciling your figures easier.

To zero the tax codes you can use the **VAT Transfer Wizard**, this avoids you having to create the journal entry manually.

You must keep all your reports and work on the VAT Return and its reconciliation for inspection by the C&E.

Reports

This section of the program enables you to alter or display the default reports or you can create your reports, in whatever layout and with the contents you want.

To create a new report, click the **New** button on the **Reports** toolbar, you will be given a choice.

You can also create new reports within the report section of the individual modules (e.g. Customers, Suppliers, etc.).

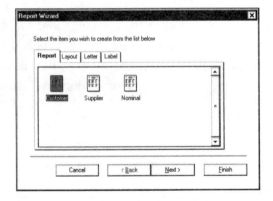

You will then be taken through the **Reports Wizard**. You will be asked to enter data and choose which fields you want to include within the report.

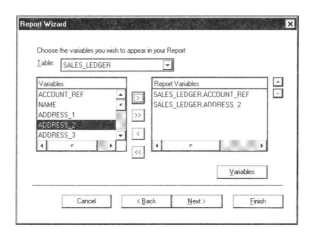

Finally the report layout will be displayed (which you can alter by adding/deleting text and fields). You save the report and then use it whenever you wish, it will be stored in the appropriate folder and appear on the relevant list. I created a new customer report called **NEWCUST** and it appears within the list of customer reports.

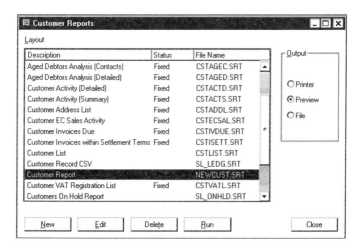

Tasks

Use this to set up a list of tasks that you need to do and view any tasks that are due, overdue or completed.

You can also set up bills that are due and so on, the variety of tasks is shown on the left of the initial screen shown below.

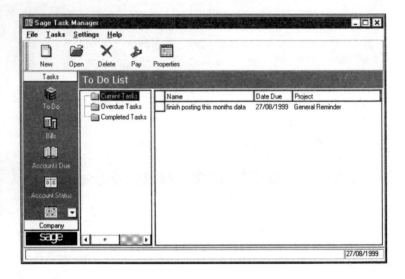

Internet

This connects you to the Sage Internet site; your browser will be loaded together with a link to the Sage site.

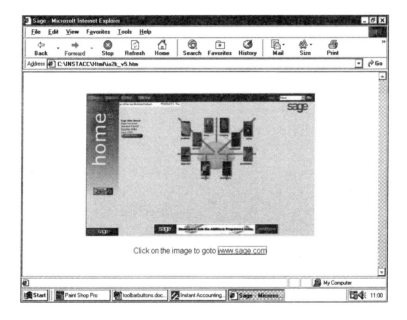

Wizards

This displays the various wizards available within the program.

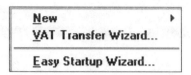

The **New** button leads to a further menu, which displays more wizards.

Help

As with all Windows programs, there is a help button. The various options were explained earlier.

The Tutorial

Preliminary tasks

Before you can begin the exercises, you need to carry out certain tasks.

Rebuilding (clearing) the data

Initially, you need to clear all the previous data (**after backing it up if necessary**) by pulling down the **File** menu and selecting **Maintenance**.

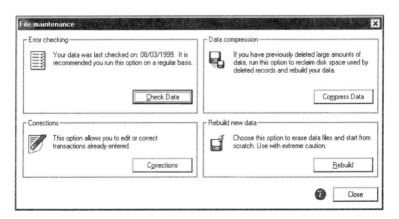

Click the **Rebuild** button.

Make sure all the ticks are removed from the boxes and
this will rebuild your data files and clear all the existing
data.

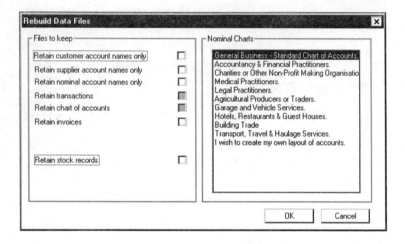

Next you will be prompted for the financial year, set it to
January 1999.

Close all the open windows.

The Easy Startup Wizard

Click on the **Wizards** button (you may need to scroll to the right to see it) and then select **Easy Startup Wizard**.

Follow through the screens, clicking **Next**, adding or altering the screens as described. If no changes are shown, accept the default settings.

Company Records

The wizard enables you to set the defaults for your business (most of which can be altered later).

These deal with information about your business.

Enter the data shown (if applicable).

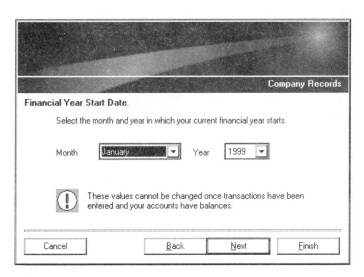

Company Records

Financial Year Start Date.

Select the month and year in which your current financial year starts.

Month [January ▼]   Year [1999 ▼]

⚠ These values cannot be changed once transactions have been entered and your accounts have balances.

[Cancel]   [Back]   [Next]   [Finish]

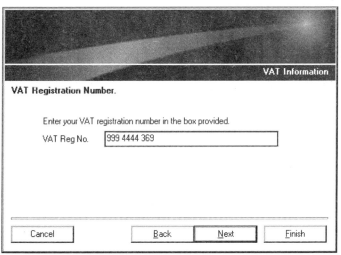

VAT Information

VAT Registration Number.

Enter your VAT registration number in the box provided.

VAT Reg No. [999 4444 369]

[Cancel]   [Back]   [Next]   [Finish]

VAT Cash Accounting

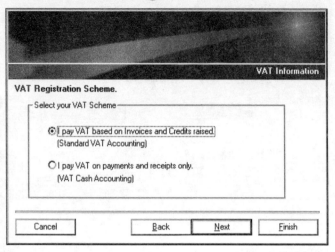

VAT cash accounting means that you pay and reclaim VAT only on the money received or paid. This differs from the standard scheme where you have to pay VAT on sales or purchases when you make the sale or purchase, **not** when you actually pay for the item or receive the money for the sale.

VAT cash accounting is designed to ease the cashflow of small businesses and if you feel it would be useful to you then you should contact the VAT office.

Customer & Supplier Information

When setting up the defaults for your customers and suppliers, you can alter the settings, e.g. ageing periods, account terms, nominal codes and VAT rates.

The defaults are set as the standard for all customers and suppliers; you can change individual customer or supplier details (within the respective modules).

The idea is that if much of the information is common then you can enter it here and avoid having to enter it for every individual customer or supplier.

Set the **Payment Due Days** to 30 (days) for both suppliers
and customers (as shown).

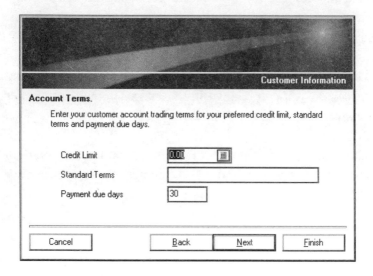

Finally view the remaining screens and **Finish** the wizard.

Sales Ledger

The Sales Ledger (called **Customers** within Sage) is used to record (credit) sales made to customers.

A credit sale is when the goods or services are supplied and an invoice is sent to the customer for payment later (normally within a month).

The basic data entered into the Sales Ledger is:

❖ Customers' Names, Addresses and other necessary details.

❖ Details of the invoices sent to customers for goods or services supplied.

Each customer is allocated a separate account (sometimes more than one, for example, if there are different branches) and each account is given its own account code.

Entering Data into the Sales Ledger

After clicking the (left-hand) mouse button on **Customers** in the main Sage screen, you will see the **Customers** screen.

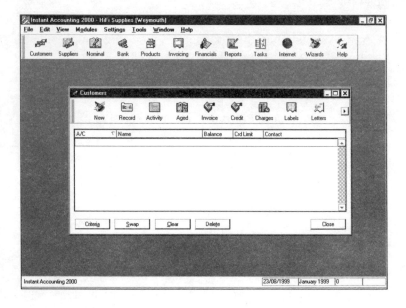

Recording Customer Details

The first task within the **Customers** module is to enter customer details (you cannot enter any other data until the customer details have been entered and saved).

To do so, click the **Record** button and the following screen will appear.

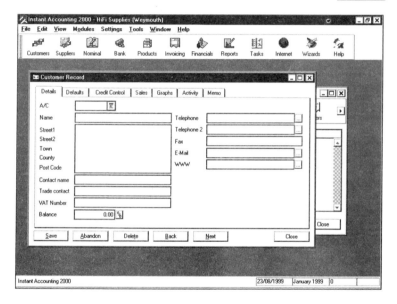

See how the screen is divided into fields, e.g. Name, Street1, etc., (each field contains a specific type of data in a similar way to a database).

You enter each customer's details within this screen.

If you do not want to enter data into a particular field use the **TAB** key to move to the next field (or click the mouse pointer within the next field).

You **must** save each record before moving onto the next; this is done by clicking on the **Save** button along the bottom of the screen.

If you make a mess and want to start again just click the **Abandon** button.

You are going to enter two customers.

Customer Data to be entered

A/C	ADAMS	CANDY
Name	Adams Electrical	HiFi Store
Street1	33	Hilltops
Street2	High Street	New Road
Town	Somerton	Taunton
County	Somerset	Somerset
Postcode	TA34 6FT	TA1 6RD
Contact	Joe Adams	Susan Smith
VAT no	444 7774 666	212 5555 456
Telephone	01786 234512	01653 87878
For both, select the **Credit Control** tab and tick the **Terms agreed** in the **Restrictions** section		

The **A/C Code** has to be different for each customer and can be numeric, alphabetic or a mixture.

It pays to think carefully about how to structure the codes to maximise efficiency and to allow additional customers to be added at a later stage (thus numbering them 1, 2, 3, etc., would cause problems if you wanted to insert a new record between 2 and 3).

You can also set up new customers using **New** button that loads the wizard (although this can be a slower method).

When you have finished entering both customers, click on the **Close** button and return to the Customers screen.

After returning to the **Customers** screen, you will see the two customers listed (as shown below).

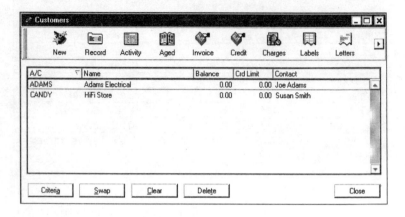

So far, you have entered details of two customers.

The next stage is to enter invoices sent to the customers.

To the right of the **Record** button is the **Invoice** button.

This is used to enter details of goods or services you have supplied to customers.

Click the **Invoice** button and you will see a new screen.

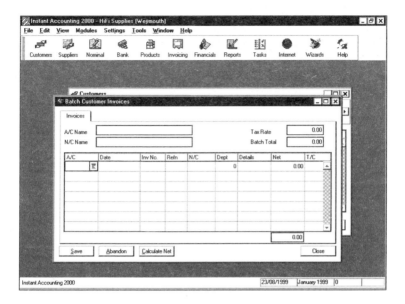

Note the button next to the **A/C** field. This appears within many of the Sage screens. If you click on it, you will see a list of the available data.

Entering Invoice Details

You are going to enter details of two items sold to CANDY.

Some of the data (e.g. the Customer Name) is automatically entered by the program once you have entered the A/C code.

The date can be entered manually or you can use the calendar (by clicking the button).

Accept the **VAT code** as **T1**, this is the default code and is set at the standard rate of VAT (the VAT will be calculated automatically).

Accept the data already entered, e.g. the nominal codes; only add (or alter) the data as required.

Save the invoices by clicking on the **Save** button and click on the **Close** button to return to the main **Customers** screen.

Customer Invoice data to be entered

Both invoices can be entered on the same screen.

You can use the **F6** key to repeat data from the previous line.

A/C (account code)	CANDY	CANDY
Date	01/01/99	09/01/99
Ref	Candy1	Candy2
Description	Aiwa Personal Stereo	Panasonic Personal Stereo
Net	40.00	30.00

You have now entered details of two invoices sent to your customer (CANDY).

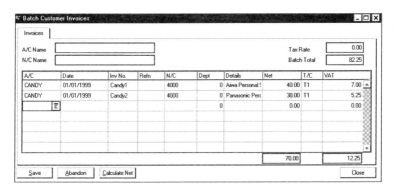

Save the data and close the window, returning to the customers screen.

Displaying Account Details

To check the accuracy of your work, use the **Activity** button to show details of the invoices and payments within an account.

Select CANDY by clicking on it so that it is highlighted, then click on the **Activity** button and accept the settings on the dialog box shown below.

Activity

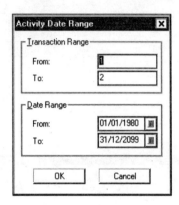

You will see the following screen, showing the invoices you have just entered.

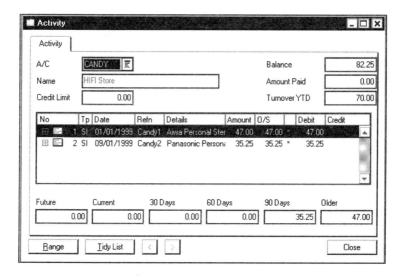

When you are satisfied, **Close** all screens, returning to the main screen. A quick way of achieving this is to pull down the **Window** menu (along the top of the screen) and select **Close All**.

You have now successfully entered customer details and invoices sent to customers. The next stage is to enter details of money received from your customers.

Recording Money Received from Credit Customers

One of the advantages of computerised accounting programs is that when data is entered the double entry book-keeping process is automatic, thus when money is received from customers, both the Sales Ledger and the Bank Account are updated.

Click on the **Bank** button.

Bank

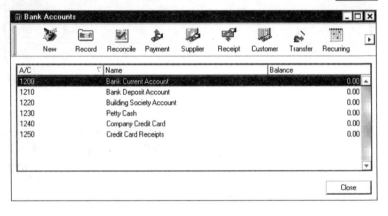

Make sure that the **Bank Current Account** is selected and then click on the **Customer** button.

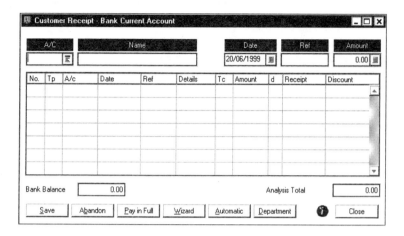

Use the button (next to the **A/C** field) to display the available account codes and choose CANDY from the list shown (clicking on the **OK** button to finish).

The screen will display all the outstanding invoices for the customer.

Alter the **Date** to the 31/01/99.

Click the mouse in the first **Receipt** column (next to the amount for £47.00).

Then click on the **Pay In Full** button.

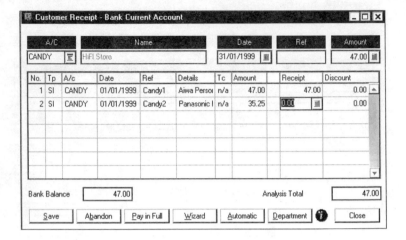

The **Amount** field should automatically show £47.00 and you can then **Save** the payment.

Finally, **Close All** the windows returning to the main Sage screen.

Again, it is worthwhile checking your work by selecting **Customers** (CANDY) and **Activity** to see how the transactions you have posted affect the CANDY account.

Your screen should look similar to that shown.

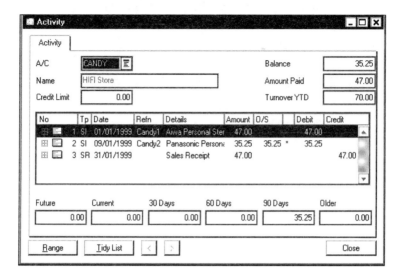

Close all the open windows.

Data and Reports

To finish this section, you can create a report showing the data you have entered.

If you highlight only one item, e.g. one customer, then you will obtain a report on only that item. To create a report on all the items, ensure that none are highlighted.

Within the **Customers** module click on the **Reports** button (you may need to scroll across using the arrowhead button) and you will see the **Customer Reports** dialog box.

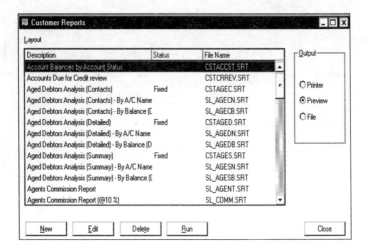

You can see that there are many reports available and you can alter some of them (**Edit**), however the ones marked as **Fixed** cannot be altered.

Select the **Aged Debtors Analysis (Detailed)** and check that **Preview** is selected, and then click on the **Run** button.

Alter the data within the next dialog box to that shown below.

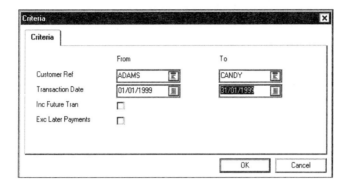

You will see the following summary of the data.

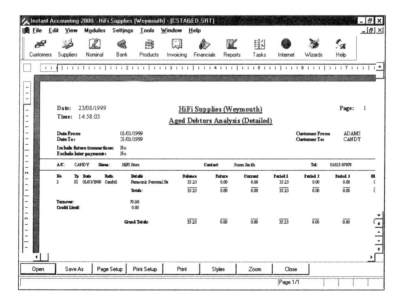

Close all the open windows.

Backing up Your Data

It is best to back up your data files regularly; you will be prompted to do so when exiting the program.

Alternatively you can back up at any time by pulling down the **File** menu and selecting **Backup**.

The first screen you see is shown below.

Click the **Setup** button and then choose the **A:** drive (or whatever drive/folder you wish to back up to), clicking **OK** when you have selected the correct drive.

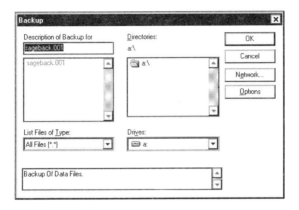

Finally click on **OK** to back up your files.

There is a considerable difference between **Backup** and **Restore**.

Summary

So far you have learnt to:

❖ Record details of customers (Record)

❖ Enter invoices into the ledger (Invoices)

❖ Record money received from customers (Bank)

❖ Look at the transactions within a customer account (Activity)

❖ Print out a report (Reports)

❖ Back up your data to a floppy disc (Backup)

Your next step is to practise what you have learnt so far.

Remember to look back if you are unsure.

New data (Customers)

Enter details of a new customer into the ledger.

A/C	MFIRST
Name	Music First
Street1	56B
Street2	Jeremy Street
Town	Bridgewater
County	Somerset
Postcode	TA9 7TR
Contact	Bill Baggins
VAT no	963 2541 777
Telephone	01678 43987
Select the **Credit Control** tab and tick the **Terms Agreed** in the **Restrictions** section	

Enter the following invoices to your customers.

A/C	ADAMS	CANDY
Date	07/01/99	10/01/99
Ref	AD1	Candy3
Description	Aiwa Mini System	Sony SS86 Speakers
Net	£200	£70

Enter these payments from your customers.

A/C	CANDY	CANDY
Date	31/01/99	31/01/99
Ref	Candy2	Candy3
Paid	35.25	82.25

Close all the open windows.

Check these by using the **Activity** button (in the
Customers module).

For example, the CANDY (account) should look like this.

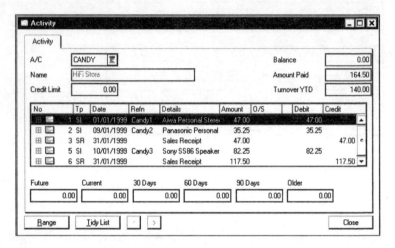

Close all the open windows.

Purchase Ledger

The Purchase Ledger (called **Suppliers** within Sage) is used to record credit purchases.

A credit purchase is when the goods or services are supplied to you and an invoice is received for payment later (normally within a month).

The basic data entered into the Purchase Ledger is:

❖ Suppliers' Names, Addresses and other necessary details.

❖ Details of the invoices received for goods or services supplied.

Each supplier is allocated a separate account and each account is given its own account code.

Entering Data into the Purchase Ledger (Suppliers)

After clicking the (left-hand) mouse button on **Suppliers** in the main Sage screen, you will see the **Suppliers** screen.

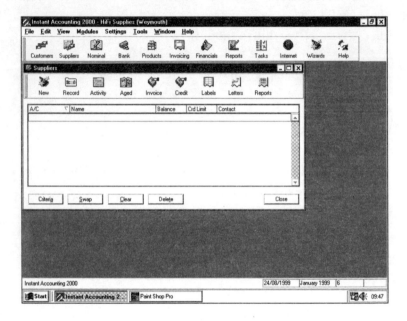

Recording Supplier Details

To begin you have to enter the supplier details. To do so, click the **Record** button and the following screen will appear.

Record

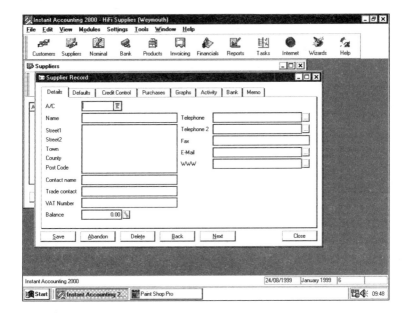

You enter each supplier's details within this screen. You **must** save each record before moving onto the next; this is done by clicking on the **Save** button along the bottom of the screen. If you make a mess and want to start again just click the **Abandon** button to begin again.

When you have finished entering the suppliers, click on the **Close** button and return to the **Supplier** screen.

Supplier Data to be entered

A/C	CHIMP	FAREAST
Name	Cheap Importers PLC	Far Eastern HiFi Products PLC
Street1	The Old Warehouse	33 Middle Street
Street2	Wareham Industrial Village	
Town	Wareham	Oldtown
County	Dorset	Shropshire
Postcode	BN45 7TR	SH5 3ER
Contact	Ilias Oldround	Oliver Ashbury
VAT No.	666 5454 222	935 4125 789
Telephone	01654 887766	01287 654391
Email	Ilias@chimp.co.uk	oliver@fareast.demon.co.uk
WWW	www.chimp.co.uk	www.fareast.demon.co.uk
For both, select the **Credit Control** tab and tick the **Terms Agreed** in the **Restrictions** section		

In a similar way to the Customers module, you can enter this data using the **New** button, which loads the wizard, but this may be slower.

New

After returning to the **Supplier** screen, you will see the supplier listed (as shown below).

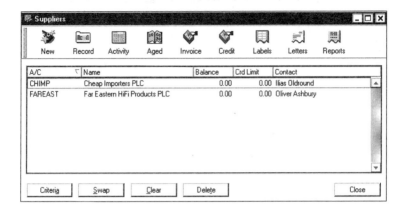

So far, you have entered details of suppliers into the Purchase Ledger.

Entering Invoice Details

The next stage is to enter invoices received from your suppliers.

To the right of the **Record** button is the **Invoice** button.

This is used to enter details of goods or services you have purchased.

Click the **Invoice** button and you will see a new screen.

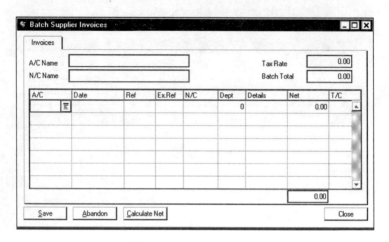

You are going to enter details of items purchased.

Note the magnifying glass button next to the **A/C** field.

If you click on it, a list of the available data will be shown and you can then select from this list.

You can enter the date manually or use the calendar (by clicking the button).

Accept the **VAT code** as **T1**, this is the default code and is set at the standard rate of VAT (the VAT will be calculated automatically).

Supplier Invoice Data to be entered

A/C (account code)	CHIMP	FAREAST
Date	01/01/99	01/01/99
Ref	Jan	Jan
Description	20 Aiwa personal stereos	30 Panasonic personal stereos
Net	£400.00	£450.00

You can use the **F6** key to repeat data from one cell to another; this can speed up data entry considerably.

Save the invoices by clicking on the **Save** button and click on the **Close** button to return to the main **Supplier** screen.

You have now entered details of two invoices sent from your suppliers.

Displaying Account Details

To check the accuracy of your work, you can view details of the invoices and payments within an account.

Select FAREAST (by clicking on it so that it is highlighted), then click on the **Activity** button and accept the settings on the dialog box shown below.

Activity

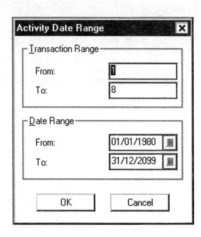

The following screen is displayed, showing the invoice you have just entered.

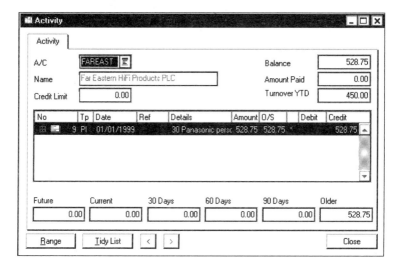

When you are satisfied, **Close** all screens, returning to the main screen.

You have now successfully entered supplier details and invoices received.

Recording Money Paid to Suppliers

The next stage is to enter details of money paid to your suppliers.

To start this process, click on the **Bank** button.

Make sure that the **Bank Current Account** is selected and then click on the **Supplier** button.

Use the button (next to the **Payee** field) to display the available supplier codes and choose CHIMP from the list shown (clicking on the **OK** button to finish).

The screen will display the outstanding invoice for the supplier.

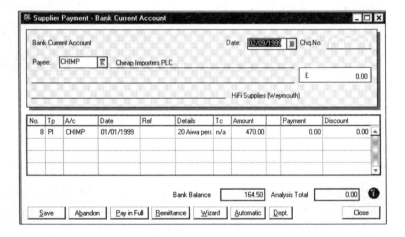

Alter the **Date** to the 31/01/99.

Click the mouse in the **Payment** column (next to the amount for £470.00).

Then click on the **Pay In Full** button.

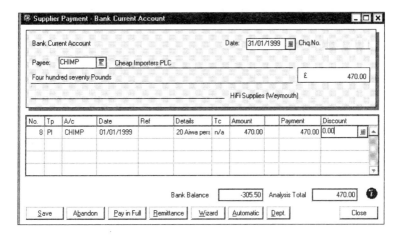

The **Amount** field should automatically show £470.00 and you can then **Save** the payment.

Finally, **Close All** the windows returning to the main Sage screen.

Again, it is worthwhile checking your work by selecting **Suppliers** (highlight CHIMP) and click the **Activity** button to see how the transactions you have posted affect the account.

Your screen should look similar to this.

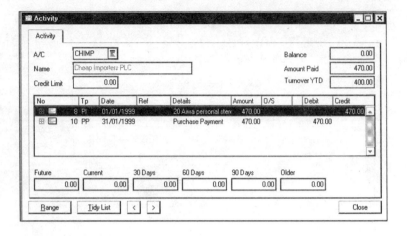

Close all the open windows.

Printing Data and Reports

To finish this section, print out a report showing the data you have entered.

Within the **Suppliers** module click on the **Reports** button (you may need to scroll across using the arrowhead button) and you will see the **Supplier Reports** dialog box.

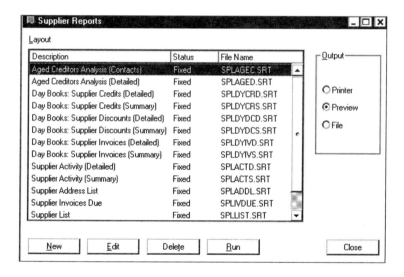

Select the **Aged Creditors Analysis (Contacts)** and check that **Preview** is selected, and then click on the **Run** button.

Alter the data to that shown below.

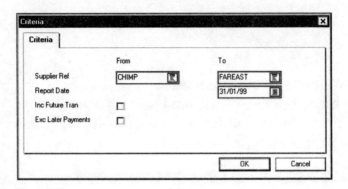

You will see a summary of the data.

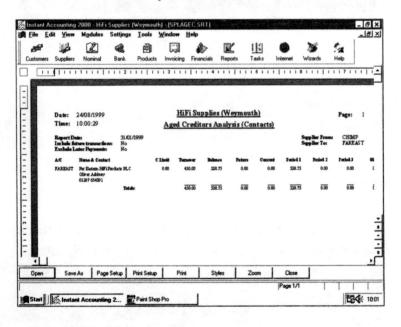

Close all the open windows.

Summary

So far you have learnt to:

❖ Record details of suppliers (Record)

❖ Enter invoices into the ledger (Invoices)

❖ Record money paid to suppliers (Bank)

❖ Look at the transactions within an account (Activity)

❖ Preview a report (Reports)

New data (Suppliers)

Enter details of a new supplier into the ledger.

A/C	CONNECTS
Name	Connections
Street1	87b Oldmile Street
Street2	Newbottom
Town	Truro
County	Cornwall
Postcode	TR7 67R
Contact	Muriel Jenkins
VAT No.	231 8547 699
Telephone	0199 54231
Email	muriel@connects.com
WWW	www.connects.com
Select the **Credit Control** tab and tick the **Terms Agreed** in the **Restrictions** section	

Enter the following invoices, saving when you have entered them.

A/C (account code)	CHIMP	CONNECTS	FAREAST
Date	20/01/1999	21/01/1999	23/01/1999
Ref	jan2	Jan	jan2
Description	15 Aiwa CD players	10 interconnects	5 Panasonic CD players
Net	600.00	100.00	300.00

A/C (account code)	CHIMP	FAREAST
Date	01/01/99	01/01/99
Ref	Jan3	Jan3
Description	Aiwa mini system	Sony ss86 speakers
Net	160.00	45.00

Close the window.

Preview the DayBooks: Suppliers Invoices (Detailed) report.

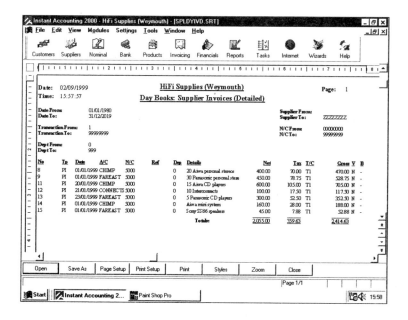

Close all the open windows and enter these **bank** payments
to your suppliers, saving each in turn.

A/C	CHIMP	FAREAST
Date	31/01/99	31/01/99
Ref	Jan2	Jan2
Payment	705.00	352.50

Finally preview the **Aged Creditors Analysis (Detailed)** -
(this is found in the suppliers module).

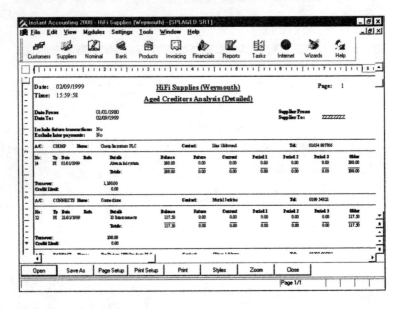

Close all open windows.

New Month - February

You have entered data for the month of January 1999, now to enter data for the month of February.

Customers Data

Enter these new customers.

A/C	TEMPLE	KENWYN
Name	Templecombe Audio	Kenwyn Supplies
Street1	89 High Street	Summerlands
Street2		SeaView
Town	Templecombe	Falmouth
County	Somerset	Cornwall
Postcode	TE4 6TT	TR8 9HG
Contact	Bill Bastins	Hugo Forest
VAT No.	555 7584 631	921 5362 845
Telephone	01654 783212	01555 621397
Select the **Credit Control** tab and tick the **Terms Agreed** in the **Restrictions** section		

Enter these customer invoices.

A/C (account code)	TEMPLE	KENWYN
Date	12/02/99	15/02/99
Ref	Feb	Feb
Description	2 Panasonic CD players	3 Aiwa CD players
Net	160.00	165.00

A/C (account code)	CANDY	MFIRST
Date	22/02/99	24/02/99
Ref	Feb	Feb
Description	4 Aiwa personal stereos	2 Panasonic personal stereos
Net	160.00	60.00

Enter the following cheques received from your customers.

A/C	TEMPLE	KENWYN
Date	28/02/99	28/02/99
Ref	Feb	Feb
Paid	188.00	193.88

Suppliers Data

Please enter these invoices from your suppliers.

A/C (account code)	CONNECTS	CHIMP	FAREAST
Date	12/02/99	15/02/99	23/02/99
Ref	Feb	Feb	Feb
Description	20 assorted plugs	5 Sony 14" T.V.s	5 Sony VCRs
Net	12.00	350.00	500.00

Now enter these **bank** payments to your suppliers.

A/C	CONNECTS	CHIMP
Date	28/02/99	28/02/99
Ref	Jan	Jan3
Payment	117.50	188.00

Close all the open windows.

Viewing the transactions

Click the **Customers** button and then the **Activity** button (making sure none of the customers is highlighted).

Accept the settings in the **Activity Date Range** dialog box and you will see a display of the transactions for the first customer account.

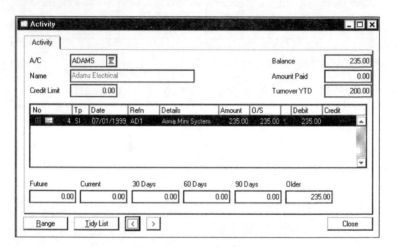

You can scroll through all the customers by clicking the arrow button.

Now look at the suppliers' activities.

Products (Stock)

You have entered information about your sales and purchases; another important aspect of your accounts is stock control.

Instant Accounting 2000 is rather limited in this area, you can record stock details and print out various reports, but you cannot record stock movements or valuations. If you want a more sophisticated stock control module then you can upgrade to Sage Line 50.

Entering Details of the Products

Begin by recording stock details. To do this, click the **Products** button, followed by **Record** and you will see the following screen (alternatively, you could use the **New** button to load the wizard).

Enter the following data (ignoring and/or accepting any fields not specified).

Save each before proceeding to enter the next.

Product Code	AIWA-MINI	SONY-SP	AIWA-PS
Description	Aiwa mini system	Sony SS86 speakers	Aiwa personal stereo
Supplier A/C	CHIMP	FAREAST	CHIMP
Sale Price	200.00	70.00	40.00
Unit of sale	one	Pair	one

Product Code	PANA-PS	AIWA-CD	INTERC
Description	Panasonic personal stereo	Aiwa CD player	Interconnects
Supplier A/C	FAREAST	CHIMP	CONNECTS
Sale Price	30.00	55.00	2.00
Unit of sale	single	single	Pair

Product Code	PANA-CD	PLUGS	SONY-TV-14
Description	Panasonic CD player	Plugs	Sony 14" T.V.
Supplier A/C	FAREAST	CONNECTS	CHIMP
Sale Price	80.00	1.00	100.00
Unit of sale	single	single	Single

Product Code	SONY-VCR
Description	Sony VCR
Supplier A/C	FAREAST
Sale Price	150.00
Unit of sale	Single

Close the **Product Record** screen and you will see the products.

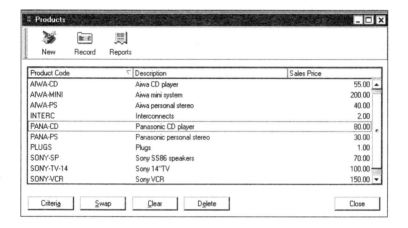

Close down the open windows.

Product Reports

Before clicking the **Report** button, be careful to ensure that you do not highlight any of the stock items, otherwise you will only get a report about those (highlighted) items.

There are a limited variety of product reports, which you can see by clicking on the **Reports** button (see the illustration below).

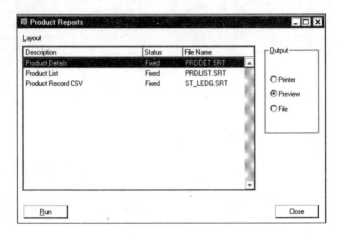

For example if you preview the **Product Details** report, you will see the details of the products listed in sequence.

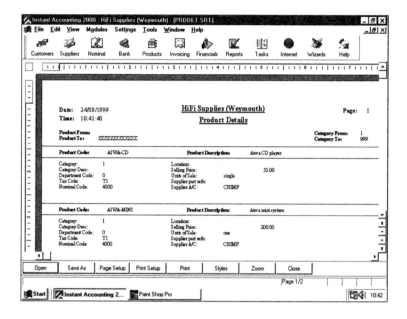

Close all the open windows.

Summary

So far, you have learnt to:

❖ Record details of products

❖ View product reports

The Financials

You have now entered data for sales, purchases and stock for two months.

The next module to investigate is **Financials**. This enables you to produce accounting statements, e.g. Balance Sheets.

One of the advantages of computerised systems will now become evident, the ability to produce financial reports without any material additional effort or time.

Click the **Financials** button.

You are going to view the **Trial Balance**.

To do this, click the **Trial** button and then on the next screen alter the **Period** to month 2, February 1999.

Trial

Check that **Preview** is selected.

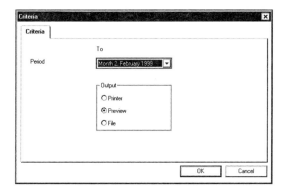

You should see a screen similar to this.

| Date: | 30/03/1999 | Hi-Fi Supplies (Weymouth) | Page: | 1 |
| Time: | 12:10:25 | Period Trial Balance | | |

To Period: Month 2, February 1999

N/C	Name	Debit	Credit
1100	Debtors Control Account	493.50	
1200	Bank Current Account		1,286.62
2100	Creditors Control Account		1,594.48
2200	Sales Tax Control Account		154.88
2201	Purchase Tax Control Account	510.48	
4000	Sales Type A		885.00
5000	Materials Purchased	2,917.00	
	Totals:	3,920.98	3,920.98

Close all the open windows.

153

The Trading, Profit & Loss Account

It is now a simple matter to produce the accounts, click on the **Financials** button and then on the **P and L** button

Alter the periods on the following screen as shown.

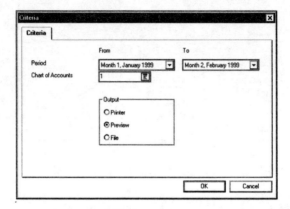

You should now see the profit and loss account for the two-month period.

Date: 24/08/1999		HiFi Supplies (Weymouth)			Page: 1	
Time: 11:25:27		Profit & Loss				
From: Month 1, January 1999						
To: Month 2, February 1999						
Chart of Accounts:		Default Chart of Accounts				
		Period		**Year to Date**		
Sales						
Product Sales		885.00		885.00		
			885.00		885.00	
Purchases						
Purchases		2,917.00		2,917.00		
			2,917.00		2,917.00	
Direct Expenses						
			0.00		0.00	
	Gross Profit/(Loss):		(2,032.00)		(2,032.00)	
Overheads						
			0.00		0.00	
	Net Profit/(Loss):		(2,032.00)		(2,032.00)	

Balance Sheet

To display the Balance Sheet, click the **Balance** button and select the same periods as the Profit and Loss Account.

The previewed result should look like this.

| Date: 24/08/1999 | HiFi Supplies (Weymouth) | | Page: 1 |
| Time: 11:27:00 | Balance Sheet | | |

From:	Month 1, January 1999		
To:	Month 2, February 1999		
Chart of Account:	Default Chart of Accounts		

	Period		Year to Date	
Fixed Assets		0.00		0.00
Current Assets				
Debtors	493.50		493.50	
VAT Liability	355.60		355.60	
		849.10		849.10
Current Liabilities				
Creditors : Short Term	1,594.48		1,594.48	
Bank Account	1,286.62		1,286.62	
		2,881.10		2,881.10
Current Assets less Current Liabilities:		(2,032.00)		(2,032.00)
Total Assets less Current Liabilities:		(2,032.00)		(2,032.00)
Long Term Liabilities		0.00		0.00
Total Assets less Total Liabilities:		(2,032.00)		(2,032.00)
Capital & Reserves				
P&L Account	(2,032.00)		(2,032.00)	
		(2,032.00)		(2,032.00)

Close all the open windows.

Summary

In this section you have learnt to:

❖ Produce the trial balance

❖ Produce the Trading, Profit & Loss Account

❖ Produce a Balance Sheet.

New Month (March)

More on Customers and Suppliers

You have entered details of purchases and sales of stock and have recorded the stock itself.

Normally you will want to set up supplier and customer accounts for as many of your customers and suppliers as possible so that you can take advantage of the many reports, etc., that can be accessed from the **Customers** and **Suppliers** modules.

Examples of such items are garage bills, motor expenses, stationery costs, professional fees and so on.

However, you may not want to set up accounts for one-off transactions, e.g. a cash sale.

To practise, set up the following **Suppliers** accounts.

A/C	JCMOTORS	ULTSTAT
Name	Jacob Cornish Motor Company	Ultimate Stationery Company
Street1	45 Chesire Street	Unit 4
Street2		Harbourside Industrial Park
Town	Weymouth	Weymouth
County	Dorset	Dorset
Postcode	DO8 9TR	DO5 6TR
Contact	Jacob Cornish	Christiana Goodenough
VAT No.	521 7898 217	564 2648 654
Telephone	02541 549874	02541 368742
Email		chris@aol.com
For both, select the **Credit Control** tab and tick the **Terms Agreed** in the **Restrictions** section		

Now record these invoices from the suppliers (note the nominal code for the invoices).

A/C	Date	Inv No.	Refn	N/C	Dept	Details	Net	T/C	VAT
JCMOTORS	05/03/1999		service	7301	0	yearly service	95.00	T1	16.63
ULTSTAT	09/03/1999		paper	7504	0	laser paper	33.99	T1	5.95

Record this bank payment (enter the date of the cheque payment as the 31st March) and close all open windows.

Tp	A/c	Date	Ref	Details	Tc	Amount	d	Payment	Discount
PI	JCMOTOR	05/03/1999	service	yearly servic	n/a	111.63		111.63	0.00

Dealing with Credit Notes

Sometimes you have to issue a credit note, for example, where the customer has returned goods.

Credit Notes from Suppliers

You have returned the **laser paper** to the supplier (ULTSTAT), as faulty.

To account for this, you need to enter the credit note.

Click on the **Suppliers** button and then the **Credit** button.

Credit

Enter the following data and save it.

A/C Name	Ultimate Stationery Company					Tax Rate		17.50
N/C Name	Office Stationery					Batch Total		39.94

A/C	Date	Cd. No	Refn	N/C	Dept	Details	Net	T/C	VAT
ULTSTAT	04/09/1999			7504		0 returns	33.99	T1	5.95

160

When you **Close** this window, returning to the **Suppliers** window, you should see the amount for the supplier is zeroed.

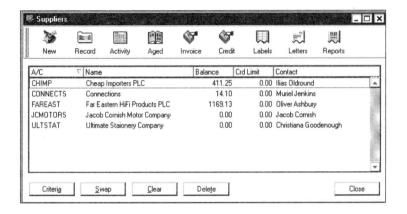

Close all open windows.

Credit Notes to Customers

Click the **Customers** button and then **Credit**.

Enter the following data (MFIRST are returning all the stock of **Panasonic personal stereos** you sold them).

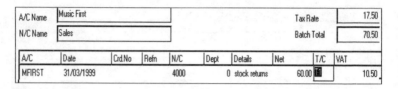

A/C Name	Music First					Tax Rate			17.50
N/C Name	Sales					Batch Total			70.50

A/C	Date	Crd.No	Refn	N/C	Dept	Details	Net	T/C	VAT
MFIRST	31/03/1999			4000	0	stock returns	60.00		10.50

Save this and close the window.

The **Customers** screen should now show the account as having a zero balance.

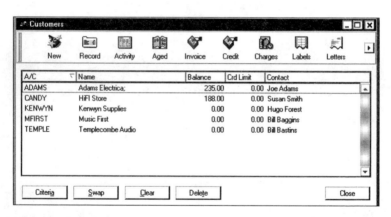

A/C	Name	Balance	Crd Limit	Contact
ADAMS	Adams Electrica;	235.00	0.00	Joe Adams
CANDY	HiFI Store	188.00	0.00	Susan Smith
KENWYN	Kenwyn Supplies	0.00	0.00	Hugo Forest
MFIRST	Music First	0.00	0.00	Bill Baggins
TEMPLE	Templecombe Audio	0.00	0.00	Bill Bastins

Close the window.

Other Receipts and Payments

There are some transactions that are not entered in the **Customers** or **Suppliers** modules as they do not have customer or supplier accounts set up for them, instead they are entered using the **Bank** module.

Payments

Use this option to record payments you make that do not involve a supplier account, e.g. payments made from your bank, cash or credit card accounts, examples are wages or miscellaneous payments (e.g. credit card company charges).

Receipts

Used to record money you receive that is not in payment for invoices sent to customers, e.g. cash sales.

Entering (Cheque) Payments

Click the **Bank** button and from the next window select **Payment**.

Enter the data shown below, saving when finished.

Note the changes to the **N/C** (nominal code) and the **Tc** (VAT tax codes).

Bank	Date	Ref	N/C	Dept	Details	Net	Tc	Tax
1200	05/03/1999	wages	7005	0	casual wages	45.00	T9	0.00
1200	16/03/1999	bus fare	7400	0	travel	11.99	T0	0.00

Entering Petty Cash Payments

Similarly, enter this petty cash payment.

Bank	Date	Ref	N/C	Dept	Details	Net	Tc	Tax
1230	23/03/1999	cleaning	7801	0	polish	3.83	T1	0.67

Save this and close all the open windows.

Recording Bank Receipts

Select the **Bank** module and then **Receipt**. Enter these receipts.

Receipt

See how you can enter receipts for different (bank or cash) accounts on the same data entry form (this applies to payments as well).

Bank	Date	Ref	N/C	Dept	Details	Net	Tc	Tax
1200	08/03/1999	sale	4000	0	pana pers ster	30.00	T1	5.25
1230	26/03/1999	sale	4000	0	2 plugs	2.00	T1	0.35

Close all open windows.

Transferring Money

It is often necessary to transfer money from one account to another, e.g. from the current bank account to petty cash.

To do this, click the **Bank** button and select **Transfer**.

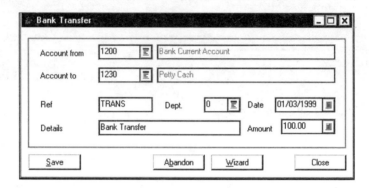

Enter the data as shown above and **Save** it.

This creates a journal entry recording the transfer of the money from one account to the other.

You should now see the following balances.

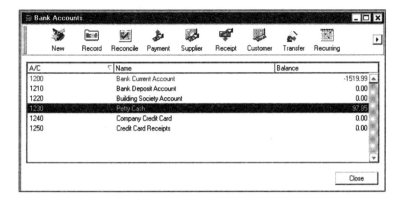

Close all the open windows.

Summary

In this section you have learnt to:

❖ Account for credit notes.

❖ Record bank and cash receipts (and payments)

❖ Record transfers between bank accounts.

End of Period Activities

You printed out various reports for the second period (month 2 - February), you are going to do the same for the 3rd month (March) and also to look at some new reports.

The VAT Return

Most businesses are registered for VAT and Sage Instant Accounting 2000 will produce your VAT return without any real effort on your part.

To do this, click the **Financials** button and then **VAT**. You will see the following screen.

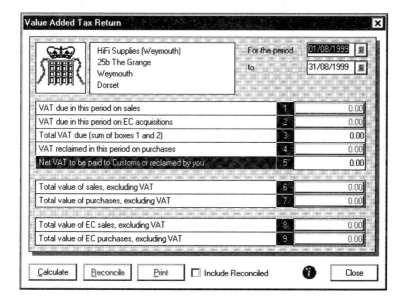

Alter the dates as shown (on the next page) and click the **Calculate** button.

The end result should be similar to this.

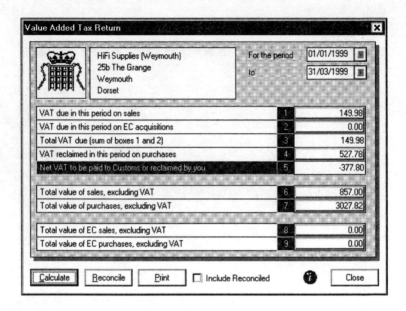

Finally, click the **Reconcile** button (this flags the items that have been included).

At this stage you should transfer the VAT liability from the Sales and Purchase Tax Control Account to the VAT Liability Account (so that the Control Accounts are zeroed to begin the new VAT period).

You use a **Wizard** to do this, click the **Wizards** button, select the **VAT Transfer Wizard** and follow through the screens.

The 2nd screen asks you to confirm the nominal code.

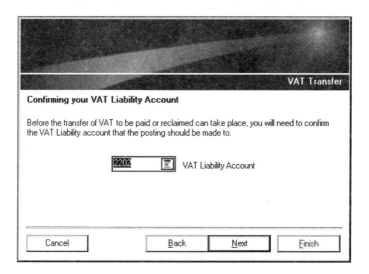

Change the date on the 3rd screen to 31/03/99 and confirm the amounts (from the VAT return you have just completed).

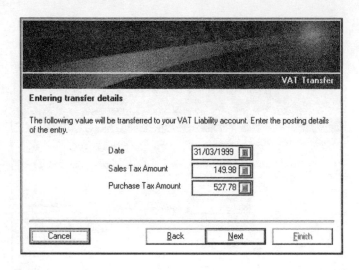

The final screen shows the journal entries that will be made.

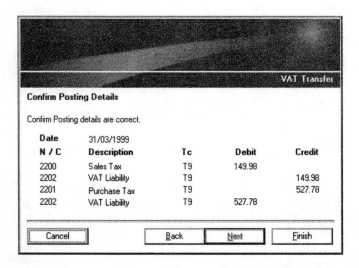

Accept these if you agree with them and **Finish** the wizard.

You have now transferred the sales and purchase VAT to the VAT Liability account.

Close any open windows.

The Trial Balance

If you now click **Financials** button and the **Trial** (Month 3 - March) you will see the revised trial balance, the Sales and Purchase Tax Control Accounts have disappeared (as they contain zero balances).

Date:	24/08/1999		HiFi Supplies (Weymouth)		Page:	1
Time:	12:05:03		Period Trial Balance			

To Period: Month 3, March 1999

N/C	Name	Debit	Credit
1100	Debtors Control Account	423.00	
1200	Bank Current Account		1,519.99
1230	Petty Cash	97.85	
2100	Creditors Control Account		1,594.48
2202	VAT Liability	377.80	
4000	Sales		857.00
5000	Purchases	2,917.00	
7005	Wages - Casual	45.00	
7301	Repairs and Servicing	95.00	
7400	Travelling	11.99	
7801	Cleaning	3.83	
	Totals:	3,971.47	3,971.47

Close the open windows.

Looking at the data

As you have seen there are many ways in which you can view the information.

The time saved by having this information easily available is material and is one of the major selling points of this kind of program.

You are now going to investigate more of these.

Customers Data

One of the ways in which you can control your cashflow (and consequently your overall business finances) is by ensuring that your customers pay you promptly.

You can see how much you are owed by your customers and importantly, how long the money has been outstanding by using the **Aged** displays.

Initially click the **Customers** button and then the **Aged** button. Alter the dates to those shown below.

You should see a display like this.

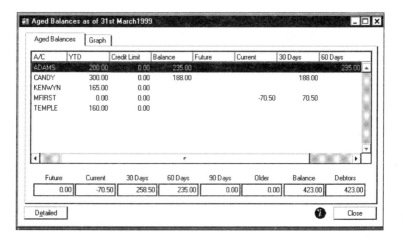

> With any date dependent report, the allocation of the balances to the periods depends upon the system date at the time of viewing the report.

As you can see, the debts are shown by period and in total, this type of display enables you to have far more control over your debtors. Close the open windows.

Financial Reports

Your accountants should want to see the **Audit Trail**; this is a list of **all** the transactions that have been entered (including any corrections).

Click the **Financials** button and then **Audit**. You want the **Summary** report. On the **Criteria** screen, accept the default entries. The report should look like this.

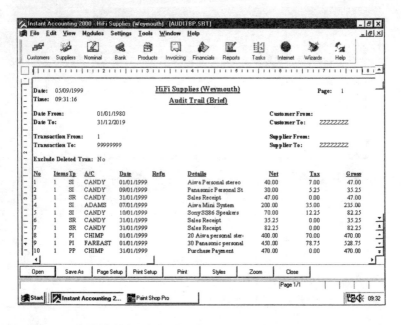

Close all open windows.

Invoicing

You can generate invoices to your customers easily by using the **Invoicing** module. You can also update the sales ledger balances automatically from the invoice details.

Click on the **Invoicing** button, followed by the **Product** button and enter the following details in the dialog box that appears (use the buttons to pull down the list of A/C References and Product Codes and remember to alter the date).

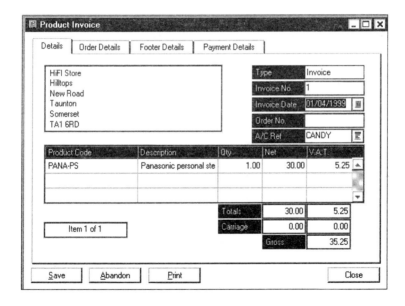

Save this and then click the **Update** button. Make sure that you have selected **Preview** and you should see the following display.

Update

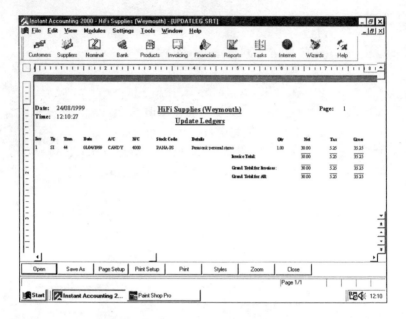

This will automatically update the sales ledger and if you look at the **Activity** screen for the customer (CANDY) you will see the item appear as the final entry.

Setting up Sage for the first time

Setting up Sage

When you set up Sage for the first time, there are various tasks you need only do once. These include:

❖   Entering your company details

❖   Setting the financial year

❖   Renaming and/or altering the nominal codes

In addition, if an existing business is transferring to Sage

❖   Entering your customers and suppliers details and amounts owed

❖   Entering the opening balances (opening trial balance)

Most of these can be carried out using **Wizards**.

Rebuilding your data files

You are going to practise these tasks using dummy data; it is vital that you **REBUILD** your data files **before** and **after** this practice.

This a totally separate exercise to the one earlier in the book and when beginning (and ending) each you should **REBUILD** your data files to remove all the practice data after backing up if you want to keep the data.

If you cannot remember how to rebuild the data, look back to the relevant section.

Easy Startup Wizard

You would normally run the Easy Startup Wizard to set up the accounts and other default data. If you worked through the earlier exercises, then this data should still be there, if not then go back to the original exercise and work through the material on the Easy Startup Wizard.

Customising the Nominal Codes

The default nominal codes can be altered to fit with your company's business.

It is one of the strengths of modern accounting programs that you can easily customise the codes to suit your own personal needs, previously if you needed to do this you would have had to purchase a bespoke program written purely for your business at great expense.

To Change the Name of a Nominal Code

Click the **Nominal** button and then **Record**. You will see the following screen, type in the code you want to alter and make the necessary changes, **saving** each before moving onto the next.

Nominal

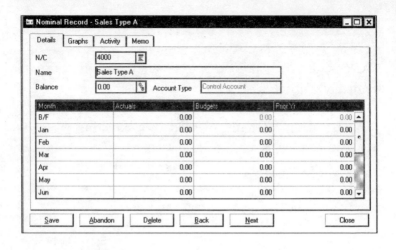

Make the following changes to the codes.

0020	Test Equipment
0021	Test Equipment Depreciation
3000	Capital
4000	Sales
4001	Sales - Connectors
5000	Purchases
5001	Purchases - Connectors
7600	Solicitors Fees
7601	Accountancy Fees

Close down the open window returning to the **Nominal Ledger** window.

Delete the following codes (as they are no longer necessary).

You can do this globally by clicking all the required codes
and then clicking the **Delete** button.

0010	Freehold Property
0011	Leasehold Property
1002	Work in Progress
1003	Finished Goods

You can enter them again by using the **Record** button (they
are reinstated when you rebuild your files).

You should now see the altered codes.

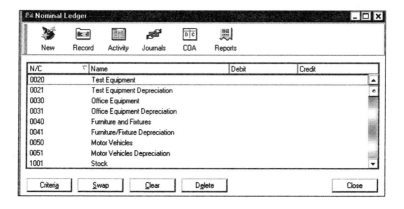

Altering the Chart of Accounts (COA)

You can add new codes to the list, however be very careful to make sure that they are within the correct category for the type of account, e.g. all overheads are between code 7000 and 9999.

You can see the display by clicking the **COA** button and then the **Edit** button.

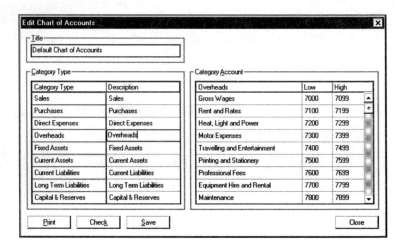

The **COA** shows the allocation of codes for each type of income and expenditure. You can alter the descriptions and the low and high parameters for each range.

Before altering the default **COA**, please be very careful indeed, only someone who knows the program well and who has an excellent understanding of accounting and bookkeeping should do this.

Close all the open windows.

Existing Customer Accounts

You need to enter existing customer accounts and record the amounts each customer owes to you.

To do this, click the **Customers** button and then **New** (this is an alternative to using the **Record** button).

Follow through the wizard, entering the data shown below.

Name	Disco Divahs	The Radio Shop
A/C	DISCODIV	RADIO
Street1	87 Ormond Road	5 High Road
Street2		
Town	Bridgnorth	Helston
County	Shropshire	Cornwall
Postcode	TL8 76Y	HE7 5E
Telephone	01658 963852	0189 789541
Email	chris@divas.freeserve.co.uk	
WWW	www.divas.freeserve.co.uk	
Contact Name	chris glidwell	alfred buttons
Opening balances (as **individual transactions** - ignore that the date is outside the current year)		
Reference	Turnt	Cables
Date	13/12/98	12/12/98
Gross	350.00	26.98

Returning to the **Customers** screen, you should see the following display.

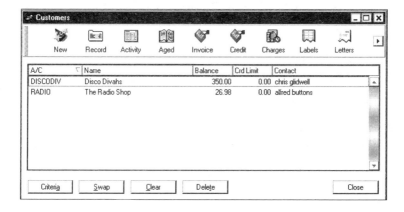

Close all the open windows.

Existing Supplier Accounts

You need to create the accounts and enter the amounts you owe.

To do this, click the **Suppliers** button and then **New**.

Follow through the wizard, entering the data shown below

Name	Japanese Co
A/C	JAPANESE
Street1	6B Yellowstone Industrial Park
Street2	
Town	Lancaster
County	Lancs
Postcode	LA9 7T
Telephone	01333 546982
Email	jojo@japan99.aol.com
WWW	
Contact Name	Joseph Jodphurs
Opening balances (as **individual transactions** - ignore that the date is outside the current year)	
Reference	Various
Date	25/11/98
Gross	265.21

You should see the following display when finished.

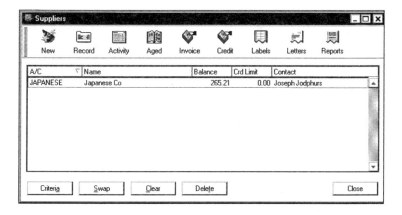

Close all the open windows.

Clearing the Suspense Account

Once you have entered the outstanding customer and supplier balances, you must clear the balance on the Suspense Account (created as a result of entering the balances). Click the **Financials** button and then **Trial**, select **Preview** (as shown below).

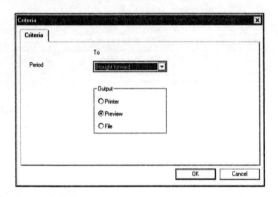

You will now see the balances shown for the customer (debtors) and supplier (creditors) invoices you have entered.

Date:	13/05/1999	HiFi Supplies (Weymouth)		Page:	1
Time:	13:22:35	Period Trial Balance			
To Period:	Brought forward				
N/C	**Name**		**Debit**		**Credit**
1100	Debtors Control Account		376.98		
2100	Creditors Control Account				265.21
9998	Suspense Account				111.77
		Totals:	376.98		376.98

To remove these balances (but leaving the outstanding invoices showing in the **Customers** and **Suppliers** modules), you need to create a **Journal**.

Journals

Click the **Nominal** button and then **Journals**.

Enter the following data (see how it is entered as the opposite of the entries in the Trial Balance, this is so it cancels out the original entries).

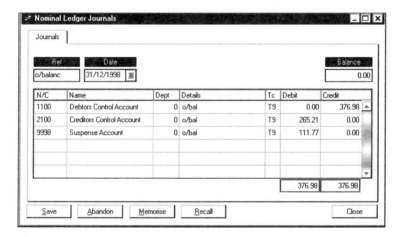

After entering the data, save it (be careful to alter the date to that shown above). This clears the nominal balances but leaves the outstanding amounts shown.

To check, click on **Customers** (and **Suppliers**) and you will still see the outstanding amounts. Close all the open windows.

The Opening Trial Balance

The information you are to enter is from your previous system (manual or computerised) and is made up of the balances on the various accounts at the end of the previous financial year.

To enter these using the journal, click the **Nominal** button and then **Journals**.

Enter the data shown below (you will not be able to **Save** the journal entries unless the journal balances, i.e. the total debits are equal to the total credits).

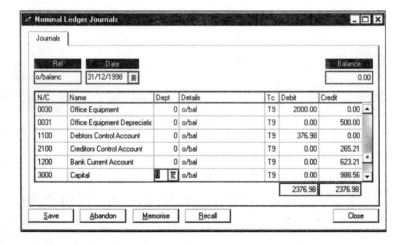

Do not worry about the messages that the date falls outside the current year, it does since you are entering the balances at the end of the previous year.

Close down all the open windows.

Now check what you have achieved by clicking the **Financials** button and then **Trial**.

Set the period to **Brought Forward** and your opening trial balance should look like this.

Date: 29/06/1999 Time: 15:53:34	HiFi Supplies (Weymouth) Period Trial Balance		Page: 1
To Period: Brought forward			
N/C	**Name**	**Debit**	**Credit**
0030	Office Equipment	2,000.00	
0031	Office Equipment Depreciation		500.00
1100	Debtors Control Account	376.98	
1200	Bank Current Account		623.21
2100	Creditors Control Account		265.21
3000	Capital		988.56
	Totals:	2,376.98	2,376.98

You can now begin to enter the current year's data.

Computerising Your Accounts

You should never install an accounting system without planning; it is not like a word processing program or a spreadsheet.

There are various ways to do this, and the following suggestions may help you plan.

It is best to install the system at the start of your financial year or at the end of a VAT period.

Setting up the coding structure requires thought. If you are unsure about this it is worth money to get a professional to help you. If you create a messy system it will be inefficient to use and costly to alter.

Always run parallel systems for a time (this means running both the old manual and the new computerised systems side by side).

Index

D

F

G

H